To Bob,

BUBBLES UP

Bouyant Adventures
in Planet Ocean

Hope you enjoy the book! Good luck to you!

Best Wishes

Paul Mila

BOOKS BY JUDITH HEMENWAY

www.divingturtle.com

The Universe Next Door

BOOKS BY PAUL J. MILA

www.milabooks.com

Dangerous Waters

Whales' Angels

Fireworks

Near Miss

Basic Underwater Photography

BUBBLES UP

Bouyant Adventures
in Planet Ocean

JUDITH HEMENWAY & PAUL J. MILA

MilaBooks.com™

Copyright © 2015 Paul J. Mila and Judith Hemenway

Published by
MilaBooks.com™
75 Titus Avenue
Carle Place, NY 11514

www.milabooks.com

Printed in the United States of America

First Edition: February 2015

Edited by Magnifico Manuscripts, LLC
www.magnificomanuscripts.com

Cover and Interior Design by MINDtheMARGINS, LLC
www.mindthemargins.com

Front Cover Photo: © 2007 Paul J. Mila (Roatan, Honduras); Diver: Ken Cross

Author Photos: © 2014 Paul J. Mila (Cozumel, Mexico);
              © 2007 Jon Fellows (Kingdom of Tonga, South Pacific)

The publisher is not responsible for websites (or their content) that are not owned by the publisher.

Library of Congress Control Number: 2015901756

ISBN: 978-0-6923-7826-7

TABLE OF CONTENTS

DEDICATIONS

Paul Mila

To my grandchildren Ava, Emma, and Max, and to any grandchildren or great-grandchildren who might yet follow. I hope you will experience your own adventures, whether above or below the waves. Challenge yourselves, seek your destinies, and above all, have fun!

Judith Hemenway

First and foremost, to Jon: my love, my partner, and my dive buddy for the past 41 years. As I write this dedication, I am still recovering from the jet lag of our most recent trip, this time to Indonesia, where we celebrated our 40th wedding anniversary diving the reefs of Southeast Sulawesi. The only thing more extraordinary than adventuring among ocean reefs and wildlife is sharing that experience with the love of your life.

Secondly, to you, dear reader. I love the ocean passionately. I love how it makes me feel, how it changes the way I view the world, how it entertains and challenges and inspires me. Whether or not you ever go diving, I want you to have those same experiences.

So come on—let's go diving!

PREFACE

Judy and Paul

We wrote *Bubbles Up* as an entertaining and informative plunge into the fascinating fluid world of the ocean, which covers over 70% of our planet's surface. It is not a scientific treatise explaining the physics of bubble formation or why bubbles rise in a liquid solution. Whether you are a diver, snorkeler, or an ocean lover who feels rejuvenated just by walking a beach or swimming in the surf, you will enjoy our stories. If you have ever wondered how it feels to look into the eye of a giant whale, have hungry sharks bump you during a feeding dive, dive into history exploring a World War II Pacific wreck, or encounter an amorous dolphin, you will want to read *Bubbles Up*.

The title sprang from serendipitous inspiration, a seed planted in Paul's brain several years ago while reading Jimmy Buffett's entertaining autobiography, *A Pirate Looks at Fifty*, published by Random House Publishing Group, 1998. In one chapter, Jimmy, a skilled pilot, described training he had previously received in the U.S. Navy's water survival school as a requirement for a ride in an F-14 Tomcat. One exercise entailed strapping Jimmy into a cockpit-sled that slid down inclined rails, "crashed" into the water, and flipped upside down. He had to hold his breath while hanging upside down, exit, and escape to the surface.

Just before Jimmy's plunge into the pool, his friend sensed his anxiety about finding his way to the surface. He slapped Jimmy's helmet and shouted an orientation tip. "Remember rock star, bubbles up!"

The phrase "bubbles up" fits the mood of our stories the way a comfortable, soft, leather glove fits your hand. And when we mentioned *Bubbles Up* to anyone who inquired about our current writing project, everyone liked it because it seems that everyone likes bubbles.

Divers like bubbles. Gliding weightless through the blue void, we sometimes enjoy watching the bubbles expelled by our fellow divers. Leaving the regulator, the bubbles expand as they rise and resemble silvery, spastic, dancing jellyfish, shimmering as they approach the surface and merge, in their last gasp, with the planet's vast atmosphere. Occasionally, we don't realize a diver is directly below us until his or her rising bubbles envelop us in a momentary glittery massage, tickling us as they pass on their upward journey.

Shimmering Bubbles   Nick Fittipaldi, Dive #2000, Cozumel, Mexico
Photo Courtesy of Miguel Núñez ©

But divers aren't the only people who enjoy bubbles. Landlubbers do, too. Remember children's parties, when each child was given a jar of bubbles and a plastic bubble wand? Even the adults watched, mesmerized, as the children's liquid creations floated away, over fences, trees, and homes. The good witch Glinda in *The Wizard of Oz* arrived on screen in her personal bubble. Whenever Dorothy was in trouble, the glowing bubble would appear and our anxiety level plummeted because we knew something good was about to happen.

We hope our book makes you feel good, too, and evokes smiles or chuckles. We relate stories, not so much about fear and danger, but about the fascinating, humorous, and inspirational encounters that we and others have experienced while diving, snorkeling, or hanging out near this deep blue world we love. While some of the stories are interrelated, they are not chronological, and we've deliberately written each chapter to stand alone. You can read them sequentially or in any random order you prefer. If you have a color e-reader, you are in for a treat: all photos in the e-book are in beautiful color.

So sit back, relax, and perhaps open a nice chilled bottle of bubbly champagne (or sparkling cider). After all, according to legend, the monk Dom Pérignon exclaimed when he first tasted champagne, "I am drinking the stars!"

And while reading our book, if you aren't sure where we're headed, just remember, *Bubbles Up*!

CHAPTER 1

WHAT AM I DOING DOWN HERE?

Paul

One sunny August afternoon, I was shopping for some vacation items in my local dive shop, Scuba Network of Long Island, where I had taken my scuba lessons. Martha, the owner, posted upcoming dive trips on a whiteboard behind the cash register. One trip in particular caught my eye as she rang up my purchases:

5-Day Trip to Nassau. Includes Shark Dive!

That sounded interesting.

"So tell me about this Nassau trip and shark dive," I said to Martha.

"It's amazing! Nice hotel, very good diving. They have several interesting wrecks, a good variety of sea life, and it's not too expensive."

"And you see sharks?"

"Oh, yes, we see lots of sharks."

Now you have to understand something about scuba diving and sharks. For all the hours that divers spend underwater, many never see sharks. After years of overfishing by this planet's number one apex predator, human beings, the sad fact is that there just aren't many sharks left in the ocean. These marvelous animals have evolved and flourished for several hundred million years. But after only about

50 years of intense fishing, humans have managed to wipe out almost 90% of the shark population. Although yelling "Shark!" will create panic and clear out the surf at a crowded beach in seconds, it's been a one-sided contest. In any single year, the scoreboard would read something like this: Sharks, 10; Humans, 100,000,000. That sobering statistic surprised me. (If you would like to learn more about this issue, search on the key words "**Sharks killed per year**" or click on this website: **http://tinyurl.com/sharks-killed-annually.**)

In the several years that I had been diving up to that point, I had seen a few nurse sharks in Cozumel, usually from a distance and only briefly. After seeing multitudes of parrotfish, tangs, butterflyfish, angelfish, filefish, and a wide variety of other sea creatures, I really wanted to see something bigger, different, and more challenging. Like sharks!

"So, Martha, do you go inside a cage?"

"No, you are right in the water with them."

"Really? And it's safe?"

"Yes, very safe. We've been on the shark dive many times. It's great fun."

"Okay. Sign me up."

What can I say? I'm an easy sell.

I enjoy photographing the creatures I encounter while diving. Undersea life is incredibly diverse and beautiful. It almost defies description. When someone asks, "What did you see down there?" it is sometimes better to show them the photos and watch their reactions than describe what I saw.

Preparing for this adventure, I learned that photographing large animals required a wide-angle lens, so it was off to the photo store. In a stroke of fateful coincidence, the salesman had done the same shark dive trip the previous year.

"Good idea buying a wide-angle lens," he said. "You'll be so close to the sharks that without using wide-angle, all you'd see in your photos are hunks of flesh. You wouldn't know if you're looking at a horse or a fish."

"Yeah? You really get that close?"

He smiled, eyes gazing off as if recalling a significant memory. "You get that close."

After a short flight from New York City, our Scuba Network dive group arrived in Nassau, Bahamas. We took a van for a 30-minute drive to the South Ocean Beach Resort on the southern end of New Providence Island. We signed the usual release forms that everyone always signs before diving.

The release absolves the dive operator from responsibility for any and all calamities that could possibly befall a diver, even if it is the operator's fault. It is so one-sided that no rational person would ever sign it under ordinary circumstances. But you're a diver, and you want to go diving. Enough said. You sign.

We enjoyed routine diving with the local dive operator, Stuart Cove's Dive Bahamas. Finally, after several days, we were scheduled to dive with sharks.

The morning of the shark dive, we were given another release to sign.

"I already signed one," I informed the dive operator.

"This one is special," he said.

I started reading the lengthy document. Like most legal documents, it was difficult to read. Stripped down to its bare essence, it basically said, *Look. You paid us to take you into shark-infested waters. You are voluntarily going to swim and dive in the water with the sharks. They have very sharp teeth. They might bite. If something happens to you, don't blame us. You asked for it. Please sign here.*

Before signing, I surreptitiously glanced at our group of 10 divers, evenly divided between men and women, to see if they were also signing the release. They were. Several had done this dive before. I quickly checked to see if everyone had all their limbs, fingers, toes, etc. They did. I signed before I changed my mind.

We left early the next morning. Our dive boat glided over a calm sea, almost mirror-like. The azure sky was cloudless; a bright sun beamed down. There was no wind. It was a perfect day to dive. After about 15 minutes, the boat slowed. We'd arrived at the dive site. Then, our Scuba Network dive escort, Mark, spoke briefly to the captain. He nodded, revved the engine, and we accelerated.

"What's up?" I asked Mark.

"I told him to take us farther out to different dive sites called Shark Wall and Shark Arena."

"Why?"

"There are a lot more sharks there than at the dive site where he was originally taking us."

"Oh, great!" I said, feigning enthusiasm but really thinking, *I'd be happy to see just a few sharks up close. I don't really need to see gazillions.*

Now we had more time to kill, pardon the expression, so on the way to the new site, the divemaster explained the dive plan. "For the first dive . . ."

"*First* dive?" I whispered to one of the experienced divers who had done this dive before.

"Yeah, the first one is to get used to swimming in the water with sharks, so you don't freak out and do something stupid during the feeding dive."

"I see. Good idea."

The divemaster continued his briefing. "We'll descend to the reef at fifty feet, swim along the bottom to Shark Wall, and then descend to about ninety feet. You'll see some sharks. They may swim toward you, but don't panic, they're just checking you out."

Why? I wondered.

"They know divers are not their normal food . . ."

Good! I felt momentarily relieved.

". . . but they're curious. They'll tend to swim at you. Don't swim away. Just face them and when they get close . . ."

How close would that be? I wanted to ask.

". . . they will turn away."

Promise? I hoped.

"They're used to seeing divers, but remember they aren't tame. These are wild animals, so don't reach out and touch them or pull their tails."

Not a chance, dude! I silently vowed.

After almost 40 minutes, we arrived at the new dive site, about 25 miles off the south coast of New Providence Island. It was located near an area called The Tongue of the Ocean, a 3,000-foot deep sea trench, home to some very large animals. There was a shallow reef, about 50 to 60 feet deep, bordering a colorful wall of sponges and coral that extended down into the abyss. We suited up. As I put on my wetsuit, I heard someone exclaim, "Hey, the sharks are here!"

What? Who's here? My heart skipped a beat, maybe two. I had expected to dive down and then find sharks. Not so. They found us first. I looked over the side of the boat, and sure enough, there they were. Several robust Caribbean reef sharks circled our boat in a slow, lazy fashion. The sun glinted off their wet, shiny, gray backs. Their dorsal fins sliced the surface menacingly. In my mind, I heard John Williams's thumping musical introduction to *Jaws*. "Dum dum dum dum dum dum."

I hadn't counted on jumping into the water and descending through circling sharks. I looked around the boat and all the divers were eagerly donning their equipment. There was a conflict raging in my mind. My brain debated with itself: advanced brain versus primitive brain. I listened passively, wondering which part would win.

My advanced, logical brain said, *Relax. Most of these people have done this dive before. They're all okay. The divemasters and photographers do it every day, 365 days a year. They're okay. Odds are you'll be okay, too.*

But the other part of my brain, the more primitive part concerned with survival, was also advising me. *Look, dummy, when you see sharks, you don't dive off the boat. You get out of the water. Got it?*

I observed the other divers, suited up and ready to dive. In the end, peer pressure and irrational macho pride won. *Sorry, primitive survival brain. I'm goin' diving!* Standing on the dive platform, suited up, ready to jump, nervously watching dorsal fins passing inches below my feet, I was very quiet, lost in thought. My survival brain had ceased counseling me. But I swore I could hear it, faintly gloating. *You'll be sorry!* The mate on the dive platform, sensing anxiety, patted my shoulder and said, "You'll be fine. Just look down before you jump so you don't land on a shark."

I stared at him. With my face mask and regulator on, he couldn't see my expression. It was the same lip curl snarl a New York commuter throws at someone who has just beaten him to the last seat in a packed subway car. I looked down again. No fins. No sharks. I jumped.

Divers do not usually descend immediately upon jumping into the water. First, we check that everything is okay. Mask is secure, regulator is in place and delivering air, and buoyancy compensator device (BCD or simply BC) vest is snug and comfortable.

But knowing sharks circled unseen a few feet beneath my dangling legs overpowered my desire for last minute formalities. I let the air out of my BC and descended. Immediately, I saw several sharks circling me. They seemed calm and unconcerned as they glided past. I wondered what was going through their shark brains as they eyeballed me. Their grace and beauty soon made me forget fear.

Caribbean reef sharks are big, not so much in length—these were 6 to 10 feet long—but in girth, husky and well-proportioned. If someone said to you, "Draw a shark," you would draw what resembles a Caribbean reef shark. They are a shark's shark. Thinking about the 20-foot-plus sharks of movie fame, you might not think a 6- or 7-foot shark is large. But trust me. Underwater, any fish bigger than you is a big fish. And if that fish has dozens of teeth, as sharp as a set of Hoffritz steak knives, it commands your attention and respect.

I looked down and saw a large, stout shark rising from the deep, considerably bigger than the others; I estimated almost 12 feet long. The other sharks scattered. I wondered if they knew something that I didn't. The shark angled straight toward me, and for a moment I forgot to breathe, violating the first rule of diving. *Never hold your breath.* I recalled our divemaster's instructions. "Don't turn away. Face the shark. It will turn away."

I aimed my camera at the shark and watched it coming closer. And closer. And closer. Every few feet I hoped, *It'll turn now, right?* I heard that damn *Jaws* music again. "Dum dum dum dum dum dum."

The shark filled my viewfinder, got to within 10 feet, and focused a black marble pupil at me. Five feet! I stopped breathing again. Then I recalled the divemaster never told us what to do if the shark doesn't turn. But then it veered slightly. I pressed the shutter and saw the strobe flash reflected in its eye. It passed over my right shoulder so closely, I felt the water displacement. The shot turned out great.

Reef Shark Rises from the Deep   Nassau, Bahamas
Paul Mila Photo ©

Discussing the photo later, my publisher termed the shot "predatory" and selected it as the cover of my first novel, *Dangerous Waters*.

We continued the wall dive according to our plan, descending to 90 feet. We focused on different types of corals, various shaped colorful sponges, and other sea life. But we were always mindful of several curious sharks cruising near us, watching us. After about 45 minutes, some of us were low on air, so we began our ascent. We stopped at 15 feet for our recommended 3-minute safety stop to reduce our chances of getting decompression illness, commonly known as the bends. We hung at that depth, one eye watching three minutes elapse on our watches or dive computers, the other eye on our escort of several sleek torpedoes, slowly circling our group. Finally, we surfaced. Knowing sharks circled under our fins raised our anxiety level a notch, and we exited the water faster than usual.

After a surface interval of almost an hour, we prepped for our second dive, the feeding dive. I felt more confident as I got ready until I noticed the divemaster, the shark feeder, and the still and video photographers donning steel-mesh shark suits over their wetsuits.

"When do we put those on?" I asked our captain.

"You don't. They're just for the crew."

"Oh." I thought about requesting a crew application. *The short form, please.* "Hey, why is the shark feeder putting on a helmet?"

"He got bit in the head last time."

"Really? Was it bad?"

"Nah, it was an accident. Just a nip."

"That's good," I replied, trying to sound reassured. *Hmmm. Did he say a nip or a rip?*

"Here's the dive plan . . ." the divemaster began.

Originally, I had thought we would descend to the bottom and watch sharks being fed from a distance, as if we were watching a movie. Wrong again.

"Follow me down to fifty feet to a shallow area we call Shark Arena. Wear several pounds of extra weight so you stay put on the bottom. We don't want you floating around uncontrolled down there. That's when accidents happen."

Accidents? What accidents? I really wanted to ask, but didn't.

"Stay in one spot. If you have a camera, hold it against your mask. Don't stick your arms out. If you don't have a camera, fold your hands across your chest. Don't wave to your buddy. If you do, a passing shark might mistake your flopping hand for a fish and bite it off."

I sure wish we had one of those nice anti-shark suits like the crew is wearing. "Once everyone's settled on the bottom, we'll bring the food down and begin feeding."

I absorbed this vital information when the still-photographer gave us her instructions.

"I'll come in front of each of you. When you see me raise the camera, it means there's a good shot of you and a shark. Don't blow any bubbles for a second so you won't ruin the shot."

The second dive began much as the first one. Look down. No shark. Jump. Get down fast.

We reached the bottom and formed a circle, about 20 feet in diameter. There were a few sharks cruising around. So far, so good. Then I looked up over my shoulder. I saw our shark feeder descending. To my amazement, more than 20 sharks surrounded him, circling the food box he carried. He reached the bottom, in the middle of our circle, and suddenly it became rush hour at Grand Central Station. Except instead of hordes of commuters, dozens of sharks surrounded us.

Several minutes into the dive, the still-photographer knelt in front of me, paused, and then raised her camera. Recalling her instructions, I held my breath for a couple of seconds. The flash fired, and I wondered what she had seen. When I saw the photo the next day, I was shocked to see the size of the huge shark that had passed only several feet behind my head, at least a 10-footer. Proudly e-mailing the photo to my friends as evidence of my bravery yielded no satisfaction. Most accused me of staging the shot in front of a screen at a Sears' photo studio. Clearly, my so-called friends regarded me as Chicken of the Sea.

I Wonder What She Saw?
Photo Courtesy of Stuart Cove's Dive Bahamas ©

The photographer moved on to another diver, and I felt someone bump me in the side. Turning to shove the inconsiderate diver out of my space, I realized it was a large shark squeezing past me to get to the food. I was grateful it preferred sushi and not prime rib. The divers in the circle were separated by four or five feet. The sharks' bodies were almost two feet wide. Add another foot or so on either side for their pectoral fins and that didn't leave much wiggle room. I heard the camera salesman's words echoing in my head. "Yeah, you get close."

The action picked up as the sharks vied for lunch. Not quite a feeding frenzy—but almost.

Where's the Fish?   Nassau, Bahamas
Paul Mila Photo ©

The sharks entered and exited our circle as they made passes at fish heads and other juicy morsels proffered on the end of a stick. Some brushed over us, rippling our hair. Others impatiently bumped us out of the way, which was extremely unsettling until we got used to it. *Got used to it?*

Despite our instructions, I couldn't resist a touch and let my bare hand brush one shark as it swept past. I felt the power of pure muscle rippling just beneath its tough skin. Some sharks cruised inches above my head, and I observed rusty hooks dangling from the corner of their mouths. Evidently, these had survived encounters with fishermen.

Continuously bumped and surrounded by sharks crossing in front, over, behind, and past me, I wondered, *What am I doing down here?* Then I pondered what would happen when the food supply ran out. I heard my damn primitive brain gloating again. *I told you so!*

Caribbean Reef Shark, Up Close and Personal   Nassau, Bahamas
Paul Mila Photo ©

To my surprise and relief, as soon as the food supply was exhausted, the sharks disappeared, ethereal forms receding into the blue gloom from where they had come. After several minutes, I couldn't find a shark on the bottom. Clearly, they keyed on the scent of the fish, not on the visual cue of the food box or us. The feeder ascended first with the empty box. The rest of us scavenged the sandy bottom, searching for shark teeth that fell from their snapping jaws during the feed. We found some razor-sharp dentures, which we pocketed as souvenirs. Several minutes later we heard a bell ring—the all-clear indicator— and we ascended, following our divemaster up to the boat. We passed a few sharks lingering near the surface.

Back on board, we exchanged animated conversation about our collective experience. Reflecting on the encounter, my breathing and heart rate were still double my normal rate. The adrenalin pumped for another hour. All my life I had read about sharks, seen them attack humans in movies, watched them rip into their prey on National Geographic Television shows, and swim repetitive paths in aquariums. But now I had actually jumped into an ocean filled with circling sharks and descended to the bottom as they swam over, under, and around me. Without the safety of a thick glass barrier separating us, I had reached out and touched passing sharks and felt their muscular bodies bump into me as they charged into the middle of a controlled feeding frenzy. This adventure was the rush of a lifetime!

CHAPTER 2

IN THE COMPANY OF GIANTS

Judy and Paul

Until recently, humans put whales in the same category as sharks: large, fearsome, aggressive creatures we must avoid at all costs because they are obviously out to destroy us. However, since we stopped hunting and started studying them instead, we've begun to comprehend their intelligence and character. Both of us have enjoyed multiple in-water encounters with these remarkable giants. Here are two of them.

Contact!
—Judy

In February of 1972, something extraordinary occurred in Laguna San Ignacio, a small bay opening onto the Pacific Ocean more than halfway down the Baja Peninsula. Two Mexican fishermen found their panga (a small, open fishing boat) surrounded by hundreds of California gray whales. For an hour, they were afraid to move for fear of disturbing the whales and provoking an attack like the one that had killed several fishermen a few years earlier. The whalers who had previously hunted whales in the bays of Baja called them devil fish because of their power and the ferocity with which they defended their young when attacked.

However, in spite of that recent attack and the fearsome reputation of the whales, and for reasons that he couldn't explain, Pachico Mayoral reached out his hand and touched the whale that hovered beneath his boat. Thus began a new era in human-whale relations. In the 40-plus years since then, word has spread, and the number of "friendlies" (both whale and human) visiting the lagoons in the winter has steadily increased.

In March 2005, on our second visit to the gray whale lagoons, my husband Jon and I and the other 25 human friendlies of our tour group had several remarkable encounters with the whale friendlies.

In Laguna Ojo de Liebre, which is about halfway down the Baja Peninsula and north of Laguna San Ignacio, our tour guides, Ecoturismo Malarrimo, divided us into three groups to board our three large pangas: *Tonino* (the panga Jon and I were on), *Susana,* and *Leviatan.* The day was sunny and calm but chilly, especially during our high-speed trip out to the main body of the lagoon. Once there, our drivers throttled back the motors to a crawl, and we spent several minutes slowly cruising and scanning for activity.

Nearby, a mom and baby approached *Susana*, and I burst out laughing at the predictable onboard chaos that ensued. In spite of having been carefully instructed by the Malarrimo staff to take turns and to keep their weight evenly distributed on the boat, all the passengers on *Susana* immediately rushed to the side where the whales surfaced, causing *Susana* to list perilously. And of course, the whales would then move under or around to the other side, and everyone would rush to that side, and *Susana* would obligingly list in that direction. Everyone reached out, shouted, and chattered in their excitement, pleading with Mom and Baby to come close, closer, so they could touch. When anyone did get a touch, there were screams of excitement, both on *Susana* and from those of us watching enviously on *Tonino.*

After a few minutes, our driver cautiously moved us in closer to *Susana.* And of course, chaos erupted on our *Tonino* as the whales approached us. We screamed. We shouted. We all rushed to one side, not the least bit interested in taking turns. We all reached out and flailed our arms. We all wanted to touch, and touch now! We spent a crazed and blissful hour sharing this pair with *Susana*. Amazingly, the whales appeared to be not the least bit annoyed or intimidated by our noise and activity. They just kept moving slowly and serenely back and forth between our two boats. Baby came up for pets while Mom lurked underneath.

I had my best contact with Baby from the back of the boat, in the motor area. When Baby came close, our driver called to me and motioned me into the back. The gunwale is lowest there, making it easy to reach the whales. Mom was huge! She came close in, but we had no contact with her. Sometimes she pushed Baby toward us, and sometimes she lifted him up. At one point, Mom swished her tail flukes **very** close to our boat as she moved toward *Susana*, but it really did look like she was deliberately careful in her movements to avoid endangering the boat. (Someone said, "Oh, she was just fluking around." So of course, "fluking around" became our phrase-of-the-day.)

Eventually, the whales tired of visiting with us and wandered off to other parts of the bay, and our driver once more cruised slowly, looking for additional action for us. Within a short time, we found a quartet—two babies playing together and two moms with them, in a shallow area with a sandy bottom. One of the moms was enormous, with a tiny baby, probably a newborn. She hugged Mom a lot, snuggling with her head against her. Once she got draped over the top of Mom's head with her tiny tail flukes slipping down Mom's side. We did not have any contact with these four, but it was delightful to sit and watch them interact. The entire setting, with the two mother-baby pairs and the shallow sandy area, reminded me so much of human mothers taking their kids to the park for a playdate.

We had very similar experiences at Laguna San Ignacio with Ecoturismo Kuyima as our guides. Our panga for this part of our adventure was *Kuyima 1*, and although its name was perhaps not as imaginative as *Tonino* or *Susana* or *Leviatan*, its ability to transport us to the marvelous world of gray whales was unparalleled. Once we reached the whale nursery area and settled in, it took only about 10 minutes before we were approached by a mother and baby. They came in together, and both appeared very relaxed and curious about us. After a while, I named the baby "Bubbles" because he apparently really enjoyed making bubbles—several times by forcing the water through his baleen while holding the side of his mouth just under the surface, and several times by blowing air slowly from his blowholes, again while just under the surface. He was small, only about as long as the boat, and his flukes seemed flimsy, so I'm guessing he was very young.

Bubbles kept surfacing, first on one side of the boat, then on the other, providing many opportunities for us to touch and pet, not to mention the opportunities to almost swamp the boat with our constant scrambles from side to side. At one point, Bubbles bumped or rubbed against the boat, as if he were scratching an itch. My friend Molly and I were together at the side when Bubbles approached.

Molly said, "Do you want me to rub your tummy?" and Bubbles rolled over on his back right next to us!

Both of us also got good eye contact with him. He rolled enough to get his right eye up near us, and we could see his eye going back and forth, up and down, taking in our faces, I'm guessing for a good 10 seconds. And then, most thrilling of all, he came straight in, nosing up to the side of the boat, directly in front of me. I leaned over and touched his rostrum gently, his dark gray skin soft and smooth and rubbery, and I could clearly see the hairs that protruded from each of his dimpled hair follicles. He held steady as I stroked and patted and communed with him. And then he slowly slipped down and away.

Even Mom came up for petting. As her massive rostrum rose out of the water in front of me, I could see that she was covered with barnacles and lice. I was completely blown away by being able to pet her. Her skin was smooth and rubbery like her baby's, but not as soft to the touch. I got a good, up-close look at the barnacles that encrusted her head and the large pink sea lice that surrounded her blowhole. And Jon actually had eye contact with her. She looked at him with her eye just a few inches underwater. Several times she pushed Bubbles

I Commune with Baby Bubbles   Laguna San Ignacio, Baja California Sur, Mexico
Photo Courtesy of Martin Anisman ©

up toward the boat, and everyone had the opportunity for multiple touches. Once, Mom's flukes sliced slowly up and sideways next to the boat, almost as if she were caressing the side, then she slipped down and away, in slow motion. That was hypnotic, magical—pure poetry.

After the first 20–30 minutes, we backed off and let *Kuyima 2* and *Kuyima 10* enjoy the experience. Mom and Bubbles thrust their heads up out of the water in a simultaneous spyhop beside *Kuyima 10*, and then Bubbles moved over to *Kuyima 2*, honoring them with several leaping, splashing breaches. I got the impression they were deliberately distributing their attentions to give all of us equal "quality time."

After about an hour, Mom and Bubbles left us, and we spent the remainder of our time observing other whales from a distance. The Kuyima staff had said that there were only about 100 whales in the lagoon at the time, but we saw maybe 20 or 30 of them, mostly mom-and-baby pairs, swimming, spouting, with occasional spyhops and breaches. Several times we saw flukes up as the whale dived deep. Lots of spouts were visible with their characteristic heart-shaped mist and that wonderful soft explosive sigh as they exhaled.

Finally, sadly, our time was up. An observation boat sat north of the viewing area and clocked each boat in and out, so time limits were strictly enforced, as was the total number of boats that could be in the viewing area at one time. Our driver Luis pointed us north toward the camp and revved up the motor.

We all had lots to chatter about throughout our lunch in the main *palapa*. Between bites of savory bean soup, cheese quesadillas, and fresh grilled fish, we relived and shared our best moments. Everyone was jazzed, thrilled, stoked.

An experience like this turns everyone into kids again, cutting through all the learned inhibitions. You totally forget to be cool or sophisticated, and it's impossible to do a head trip. Suddenly, immediately, it is Christmas morning, you're five years old, and the whole world is filled with magic.

Eye to Eye with a Humpback Whale
—Paul

Have you ever wondered what it would feel like to gaze into the intelligent eye of a 50-foot whale—as you snorkeled only several feet away? Most wildlife experts, scientists, and marine biologists would advise that swimming next to a 40-ton creature with flukes and fins powerful enough to propel itself out of the water or sink a boat is foolhardy and dangerous.

Those are my thoughts on a warm Saturday afternoon in February 2003 riding in a Zodiac, a motorized, hard-bottom inflatable 20-foot craft. Ten of us are bouncing over Caribbean waves, searching for humpback whales in the Silver Bank, a protected whale sanctuary located about 60 miles off the northern coast of the Dominican Republic. Here, the Atlantic Ocean's normally deep seabed rises to within 50 feet of the surface. Coral reefs, which occasionally break the surface, had torn open the hulls of eighteenth century Spanish galleons attempting to carry gold and silver treasure back to the Old World. Many didn't make it, sinking to the bottom and spilling their precious cargos over the reef. Hence the name Silver Bank. But the whales love the area. The relatively shallow bottom and numerous coral reefs protect the area from strong currents and waves, providing an ideal location to mate, give birth, and spend the winter. In the spring, they will venture north again to their feeding grounds in the coastal waters off Long Island and New England.

Each of us hopes to be the first to spot a blow, which signals a whale's presence. We're perched five on each side, some straddle, while others ride sidesaddle. All of us hold tightly to a rope which runs the length of the raft. As the inflatable rubber sides buckle and bend with the waves, I feel like a rider precariously perched on a bucking bronco. If you have ever bounced along on a trotting horse, you can appreciate how my lower back feels right about now.

Suddenly, one of our group shouts, "Whale at two o'clock!" The reaction in our Zodiac is electric.

"Where?" several ask, wheeling around.

"Oh, my God! I see it! There's the blow!" another shouts, pointing to a steamy geyser only several hundred yards off our starboard bow.

The front of the raft is always considered 12:00, so we look where 2:00 would be on a clock, ahead and slightly to our right. Then we all see another blow, the explosive exhalation of a whale's hot breath, condensing into mist as it meets the relatively cooler air. Our skipper adjusts course toward the whale, now less than 100 yards away. As we get closer, a thought runs through my mind: *In a few minutes, I am going to jump in the ocean and swim with a humpback whale longer than my house.*

I have seen humpback whales several times on whale-watching trips with my family, off Montauk, Long Island. Swimming majestically, backs glistening in the sun, their giant tail flukes propel them seemingly without effort through the waves. They are fascinating to see, even from the safe confines of a boat. But the idea of getting into the water with these 50-foot, 40-plus-ton behemoths never crossed my mind until about a year ago. We are close to where the whale sounded (dived to the bottom) and while we wait to see where it will surface, I reflect how my journey to meet humpback whales began.

It was an accidental meeting, while scuba diving in Bonaire a year earlier. After a day of diving, Lee Solt, my roommate for this trip, invited Ankie, a diver from Holland traveling alone, to join us for dinner. Sitting across the table, I noticed a silver whale tail hanging from a chain around her neck.

"So I see you like whales," I remarked, intending only to elicit casual dinner conversation.

"Oh yes, I love whales, especially humpbacks. In fact, I swim with them every winter in the Dominican Republic." Her reply was delivered in the same off-handed manner as one might remark, "I go to the grocery store every Tuesday to buy a quart of milk and a loaf of bread." I was stunned.

"Excuse me," I said, "You do *what* with *whom? Where?*" That simple three-part question was the beginning of my journey.

"Well," she explained, "I contact an organization called Bottom Time Adventures. They are licensed by the Dominican Government to conduct whale encounters. In the winter, usually February or March, I fly to the DR and spend a week on a live-aboard boat, snorkeling with the whales."

"And it's safe? Is that legal?"

"Oh yes, it's very well-regulated and the boat crews are very experienced."

"You're allowed to get close to them? In the water? But what about . . . ?"

As I considered the pros and cons of embarking on such an adventure, I thought about an inspirational quote from an acquaintance, Barbara Buchanan, who had borrowed and modified Hunter Thompson's original quote. Barbara wrote, "Life is not a journey to the grave with the intention of arriving safely in a pretty and well-preserved body, but rather to skid in broadside, thoroughly used up, totally worn out, and loudly proclaiming, 'Wow—what a ride!'"

And so, I decided to meet the giants.

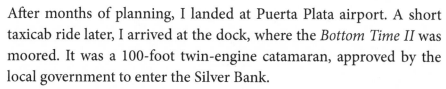

After months of planning, I landed at Puerta Plata airport. A short taxicab ride later, I arrived at the dock, where the *Bottom Time II* was moored. It was a 100-foot twin-engine catamaran, approved by the local government to enter the Silver Bank.

Twenty-one other whale enthusiasts and I spend the night in port. We are a diverse group, more women than men, from Holland, Belgium, the United Kingdom, Australia, and all parts of the United States, including Hawaii.

At dinner, we meet Captain Roger and the crew. Captain Roger explains how we will spend the next six days. "We will split into two groups of ten. After breakfast, each group will depart from the *Bottom Time II* in their Zodiac and attempt to encounter whales. The etiquette of the whale encounters is well-defined and the rules are very specific, designed with the whales' best interests in mind."

I glance around the cabin and everyone's attention is riveted on Captain Roger, mine included, listening to his instructions.

"Our Zodiacs are not permitted to chase or cut in front of whales. When we encounter a solitary whale, a group of whales, or a mother and calf, we will stop and let the whales approach. If they are interested in us, we slip into the water with our snorkel gear. Since this is a whale sanctuary, scuba is not permitted. The authorities don't want anyone harassing a whale if it stays deep and doesn't want to interact. Besides, bubble blowing in whale culture can be a sign of aggression. Trust me, folks, you don't want to piss off a fifty-ton whale."

The group laughs and one hand goes up. "How long will the whales stay with us?"

"The encounters will last as long as the whales decide. They may be as short as several minutes or as long as an hour. It's all up to the whales. After each encounter, we'll clamber back aboard the Zodiac and search for more whales. We will return to the *Bottom Time II* for lunch, and then head out again until late afternoon. That's it. Any questions?"

We all nod, indicating that we understand the ground rules of in-water whale encounters, up close and personal. The atmosphere is charged with the anticipation of meeting whales.

At 6:00 a.m. the next morning, we wake to the gentle throbbing of the *Bottom Time II's* engines. The sound soon turns into a noisy rumble as we leave Puerta Plata's harbor for an 80-mile sprint at 20 knots over the open ocean, known as "The Crossing." Those prone to *mal de mer* are advised to take seasickness medication before our departure, since we will be pounding through heavy swells.

Four hours later, we reach the perimeter of the Silver Bank, and Captain Roger reduces speed to avoid striking any whales. The *Bottom Time II* slows to under 10 knots for the remainder of our journey, and we see humpbacks in the distance. Some breach, leaping clear out of the water and crashing back in a foamy explosion. Others repeatedly pound the surface with their tails, an activity called tail slapping or tail lobbing when they strike down at an angle. Some roll onto their sides, smashing their 10- to 15-foot-long pectoral fins, the longest appendage of any mammal, against the surface, a behavior called pec slapping. The whales are greeting us with an impressive power display.

Last night at dinner we were told that if the whales exhibited these violent behaviors, we would stay on our Zodiac and seek out calmer whales. I wanted to ask, *But what if a calm whale suddenly decides to . . .* Then I thought, *Why be a killjoy and spoil the group's enthusiasm with a downer question like that?* Right!

So, here I am, waiting for a 50-foot humpback whale to surface so I can jump into the water with it, hoping that he, or she, doesn't turn out to be a breacher, tail lobber, or pec slapper. While standing at the helm, our skipper wears polarized sunglasses that cut through the surface glare and provide a better viewing angle of the ocean bottom. He breaks my meditation with a sudden announcement.

"Hey folks, looks like we might have a sleeper. The whale's just resting near the bottom. Everyone into the water quietly. Now!"

This is it! We all slip into the water splashing as little as possible. I adjust my face mask and peer underwater, scanning the bottom. I notice a mass obscuring the topography of the ocean floor, 60 feet below. I blink and focus. The mass is huge, like an island! Then, the "island" slowly, almost imperceptibly, begins moving and I realize just how big a whale is. Viewed from the surface, only a whale's back is usually visible, sometimes the full length all the way to its tail fluke. But the great bulk, underwater, is never seen. Here, I can see its girth is enormous. The whale turns gracefully, and then rises. The animal is essentially weightless in the water, but I am still amazed that something so huge can move so easily.

Our little band of 10 adventurers is spread out on the surface, and the whale gazes up at us. Is the look one of curiosity? Ambivalence? Annoyance? It circles and I am trying to absorb all the details: the enormous tail flukes, 10 feet across; the long, white pectoral fins; the graceful motion of its massive body. It continues rising, now only several feet directly under me. I am entranced, looking down at the passing head, the blowhole, and the small dorsal fin. Then, I look back and see the giant tail flukes coming toward me, rhythmically pumping slowly up and down, propelling 40 tons of whale through the water. I notice that each up-stroke of the flukes breaks the surface. Then I realize in several seconds I, floating on the surface, will be in their path.

There is not enough time to maneuver away, so I fold my arms across my chest to prevent the broken ribs I expect to suffer in a few seconds. The whale is passing below me, and I watch the tail flukes rising toward me. I brace for the impact but the flukes stop at mid-position. The whale's momentum carries it past me, and I am dumbfounded to see the flukes resume their full range of motion. Clearly, this whale knew exactly where I was relative to its own position and held its tail flukes in order to avoid striking me. In several seconds, the whale disappears into the blue-green haze and we climb back on board to exchange our experiences. I am almost speechless, but I relate my experience to our skipper. He returns a knowing smile.

"Yeah, that's what the whales usually do when they know you're there."

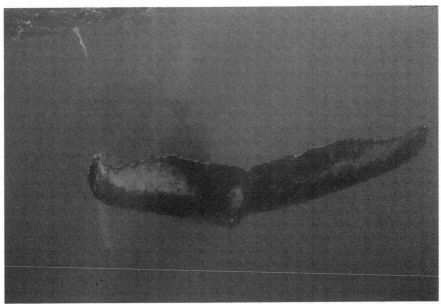

Disappearing Whale
Paul Mila Photo ©

Silver Bank Whale Sanctuary, Dominican Republic

It is late afternoon, so we return to the *Bottom Time II*. Dinner conversation is quite animated. The other Zodiac encountered a mother and newborn calf, about a month old. These are the best encounters because baby whales are curious and the experience might last for an hour or more. Encounters with adult whales are usually shorter, perhaps just a quick pass. They have seen humans before and usually have other things on their whale minds. But the 10- to 15-foot-long, 2,000-pound babies are seeing humans for the first time and are intensely curious, sometimes even playful. A mother whale will stay close, permitting the presence of humans but clearly monitoring the situation. We listen intently as the other group describes their emotional experience. We are happy for them but also a little envious. We crave the same close encounter—to look into the eye of a whale and feel a connection to another species. Well, tomorrow is another day.

Next morning after breakfast, we depart in our Zodiac, but the whales are sleeping, hiding, or just playing elsewhere in the Silver Bank. We cruise, scanning the horizon for a blow or other telltale sign indicating a whale's presence, perhaps the foamy explosion of a breach. Out of nowhere, we are suddenly surrounded by a cacophony of sound: the eerie moan of a humpback whale song. Normally, it is virtually impossible to hear their sounds above the surface. But this whale is sufficiently close that the Zodiac's hard bottom is vibrating like a piano's soundboard, transmitting the sound through the air.

"Hey, we have a singer below us!" shouts the skipper. "Everyone into the water."

We're quickly over the side, but the water is a little murky today and we cannot see the whale. Sound travels fast and far underwater, and most likely the whale is farther away than we suspected. We climb aboard, disappointed, but still amazed by the unique experience. On the way back to the *Bottom Time II*, we hope for better luck this afternoon.

After lunch, we are out less than an hour when our skipper spots two whales headed in our direction. He cuts the outboard motor and we drift silently, watching the whales approach. Gauging the distance from the tip of their heads to their dorsal fins, we estimate one is very large, 40 to 50 feet, and the other much smaller, maybe 12 to 15 feet. Finally, they are abreast and they pause. Our skipper watches them for a minute, then makes a decision.

"Okay everyone, get in quickly!"

I am one of the first in the water, camera at the ready.

The whales have descended and are resting near the bottom. One is a very large female. The other is her calf, we estimate about a month old and already weighing about 2,000 pounds. We watch them for several minutes, transfixed as they interact. The baby swims over, under, and around the mother's head, constantly touching, nuzzling, and maintaining continual contact. Then, the baby leaves the mother and suspends itself vertically in the water, seeming to stand on its tail, watching us. Finally, it ascends toward us. We are spread out in a giant crescent-shaped pattern. The whale swims toward the end-person and then closely past each of us, in turn. Baby seems taken with us, and after a first pass it circles and comes in again, this time straight toward me. It gets to within 10 feet and turns to look at me. *Eye contact!* As Baby passes, I raise my camera and take a shot.

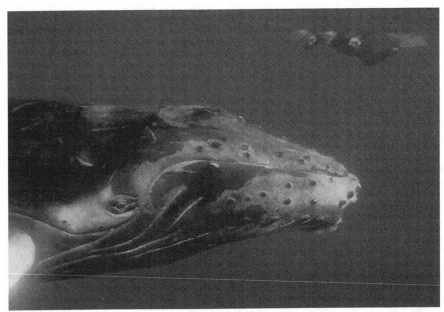

Eye Contact　　　　　　　　　　Silver Bank Whale Sanctuary, Dominican Republic
Paul Mila Photo ©

We stare at each other, but this is like no other eye I have ever seen. It is not just looking at me, but evaluating, assessing, wondering. It is an unsettling, but also wonderful, feeling. I know this baby will remember what it is seeing and will store the information in its whale frame of reference. How I will fit into that context, I do not know. As the baby whale passes, it spreads its pectoral fins and gently grazes the outstretched hand of a woman several feet away. It is an intentional, inquiring touch, gathering more information to store in its memory bank, about these strange, tiny creatures that swim with little fins.

Surfacing, our group looks at each other. The woman who was touched by the whale is crying. Others are on the verge of tears over the experience. A baby whale encounter can do that to you! After a minute, I reposition my mask and look under the surface. I see the mother coming straight toward me, slowly but deliberately.

I am wondering what is going through her mind. Getting close to an animal's offspring is not something you would attempt with most wild animals, certainly not with a bear or a lion.

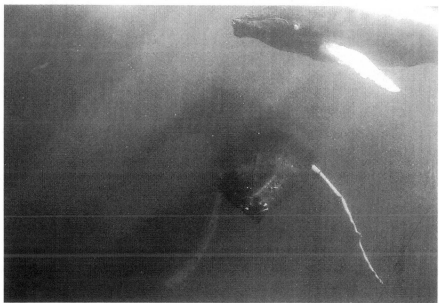

Mom Coming Toward Me
Paul Mila Photo ©

Silver Bank Whale Sanctuary, Dominican Republic

She gets within several feet of me, gracefully turns her massive body, and gazes at me as she passes. I have looked into a shark's cold, expressionless eye. Its evaluation process is very simple: Are you food, a threat, or an irrelevant part of the background? That's about it. But *this* eye is very different. Mom rotates her baseball-sized eyeball and looks directly at me, but in a different manner than her baby did, not with the same sense of wonder. Clearly, she has seen humans before. Her gaze reflects cognition, a wisdom born from eons of evolution, an understanding, an *intelligence*. We stare at each other for several seconds, evaluating each other. Is she wondering what I thought of her baby? Has she seen her kind killed by other humans, and is she wondering why we seem so different? I cannot tell. But as our eyes lock, I feel an exchange has occurred.

The whale is so close I realize her extended pectoral fin will strike me as she passes. But she draws her fin back alongside her body, avoiding contact.

I marvel at her concern for me, her respect for my personal space in the water. I reflect that this is the second time in as many days a

Mother Humpback Passes Without Hitting Me   Silver Bank Whale Sanctuary, Dominican Republic
Paul Mila Photo ©

Mother Pumping Her Giant Tail Flukes   Silver Bank Whale Sanctuary, Dominican Republic
Paul Mila Photo ©

mighty whale has demonstrated restraint and recognition of human frailness. A few seconds later, I watch her pump her giant tale flukes as she follows her baby and disappears into the blue gloom.

Our skipper brings the Zodiac to retrieve us amid our joyful shrieks and high-five exchanges. Once aboard, we hug each other over our shared experience, and then settle into individual reflection on the way back to the *Bottom Time II*. We all realize this experience has changed us in some way. No matter what happens for the remainder of the week, I am satisfied; I am happy. This is why I came to the Silver Bank—*to look into the eye of a whale!*

Several years after this trip, the *Bottom Time II* ran afoul of a hurricane and now really rests on the bottom in the company of giants.

CHAPTER 3

CHANCE ENCOUNTERS
CAN CHANGE YOUR LIFE

Paul

Have you ever reflected on how the countless personal intersections you experience and the choices you make can alter your life? How different your life is now because at one time in your past you chose path A instead of path B?

Scuba diving had always captivated me, ever since watching the underwater exploits of Mike Nelson (Lloyd Bridges) in the popular 1950s television series, *Sea Hunt,* and later watching the fascinating 1970s Jacques Cousteau specials.

My personal involvement with scuba diving started in the summer of 2000, when we and our neighbors chose to take a vacation to Cozumel, Mexico, instead of several other possible locations. We stayed at the Allegro, an all-inclusive hotel on the southern end of the island, located on a beautiful white-sand beach named San Francisco. From our beach location, we watched the daily routine of our hotel's dive operator, *Dive Palancar,* prepare the dive boats for their daily trips. Listening to the bell-like tones of scuba tanks clinking and clanking as the staff wheeled them on dollies to the dive boats moored at the hotel pier became part of our morning ritual. As we lounged under coconut palm trees, we watched a parade of dive boats taking customers out to explore the many reefs for which Cozumel is famous. Upon their return, the divers looked more than just happy and satisfied. They appeared exhilarated. I watched their animated conversations as they discussed their dives, nodding, smiling, laughing, gesticulating with arms spread wide, obviously describing an encounter with some large sea creature. I couldn't hear what they were saying, but I wondered, *What are they seeing and experiencing beneath the surface of that beautiful azure sea?*

After several days of listening to the activity coordinator announce, "Free scuba lessons, nine o'clock in the pool," my curiosity was piqued. I decided to take the plunge. The next morning after breakfast, I sat poolside with several other tourists, waiting for our randomly assigned instructor. We noticed a tall woman walking toward us. What caught my eye was her woven palm hat with fronds splayed out in all directions and her huge wraparound sunglasses. *Another crazy tourist*, I thought.

She sat down, smiled, and announced, "Good morning. My name is Alison and I'm your dive instructor."

Is she for real? I wondered. After only two minutes listening to her instructions, I realized the lady knew her material, and she was an excellent communicator who could also teach. We all listened very intently, especially when she mentioned early on that holding your breath underwater as you ascend could cause your lungs to explode, killing you. Trust me, information such as that will definitely catch your attention!

After we listened to her 15-minute lecture on the basics of scuba diving, we tried on the equipment in the pool. Alison explained and demonstrated how to breathe underwater (through your mouth, not your nose), how to flood your mask and clear it, how to recover your regulator if it came out of your mouth, how to maintain buoyancy control, and other relevant information that would keep us alive underwater.

After the pool lessons, Alison announced that we could try a shore dive, where we would go as deep as 15 to 20 feet. Of course, there was a fee for this but, after all, hooking us and reeling us in was the real intent of the free lesson. As we suited up at the shoreline, another diver joined us. We learned he was already certified but had signed up for a refresher dive. He was a paraplegic, in his 30s, who had lost the use of his legs when he fell from a ladder while painting his house. In place of fins, he used webbed gloves to propel himself through the water. I was struck by his overall positive attitude and his love for diving. He was determined not to let his disability interfere with a sport that he loved so much. His enthusiastic attitude for scuba diving made a lasting impression on me.

Our beach dive went well, and Alison found a small nurse shark hiding under a rock. She announced that we could do a boat dive on a reef tomorrow if we were interested. I was hooked like a marlin.

Looking back now, more than 500 dives later, my first boat dive with Alison on a reef called Paso del Cedral was one of the best dives I have ever experienced. We encountered a table-sized, friendly, or perhaps just curious, hawksbill turtle. As he swam corkscrews around us, I was also amazed by the sea life around me. I felt like I was swimming inside an aquarium. The diversity of fish, corals, and sponges astounded me! That dive motivated me to get scuba certified, as soon as possible, when I returned home. I took my classes and pool lessons at Scuba Network in Long Island, but I returned to Cozumel so Alison could conduct my open water dives and complete my training. So, at the "tender" age of 52, I became a certified scuba diver.

About a year later, Alison left her instructor position at the hotel and bravely struck out on her own to start her own dive operation, Scuba with Alison. I have maintained a friendship with Alison over the years and have continued diving with her whenever I visit Cozumel.

The beauty of the undersea world led me into the field of underwater photography, and I have had the pleasure of diving with, and photographing, Caribbean reef sharks at Shark Arena in Nassau, humpback whales and their calves in the Silver Bank of the Dominican Republic and Tonga, South Pacific, and a variety of sea life in Bonaire, Hawaii, Grand Cayman Island, Antigua, Roatan, and Cozumel. When I retired from corporate life three years after becoming a certified scuba diver, I decided to combine underwater photography with writing and published *Dangerous Waters* in April 2004.

Looking back 15 years later, I realize the decision to vacation in Cozumel proved to be one of those life-altering decisions. Meeting Alison was a chance encounter, one of those random personal intersections that change a person's life. For me, it opened new vistas that I had never considered before. Paraphrasing the advertising slogan of my former employer, MasterCard International, I can definitely say that diving has led me to many *priceless* experiences!

CHAPTER 4

EIGHTEEN MINUTES ON A RAINBOW

Judy

Diving in California is very different from diving in the tropics. Typically, California waters are about 20° F colder than the tropics, with rough surface chop on top of 2- to 6-foot swells and frequently plagued by strong, changeable currents. So why would anyone in their right mind ever dive in California? Join me here on a typical dive, and find out for yourself.

〜⌒

7:30 a.m. Gray. Overhead, a solid, light-gray cloud cover looms over the sea, a shabby, clotted cotton dome. Not fog. This is the almost-always-present marine layer that forms overnight when the day's air, warmed by the summer sun, meets the cold currents flowing south along the California coast—waters still cold from their clockwise journey across the northern Pacific. Usually this chill, moist layer of condensation burns off by midday, but at this hour, it shows no sign of dispersing. The ocean surrounding us is a hard steel gray, dark and glinting, its surface rough with restless quicksilver chop dancing on top of a slow, low groundswell from the northwest.

7:30 a.m. Cold. The freshening morning breeze has a distinct bite to it. This is as close as San Miguel Island gets to a balmy summer zephyr. It's early September in the Northern Channel Islands and still summer. Summer doesn't start here until about mid-July and continues into October. But at San Miguel, even summer can be brutal. The island is the westernmost of the four Northern Channel Islands, a chain of mountains strung out in the eastern Pacific, close-in and parallel to the Central California Coast. The coast runs east-west here until it reaches the double elbow of Point Conception and Point Arguello. Anacapa, Santa Cruz, and Santa Rosa Islands are all tucked in behind that elbow and protected from the prevailing weather that blows in from the northwest. But not San Miguel—it juts out beyond the Point, totally unprotected.

7:30 a.m. Floating. On board the *Peace*, a charter dive boat out of Ventura Harbor. We are about four miles northwest of San Miguel. Two miles to the east, the double peaks of Wilson's Rock spike above the surface of the sea, and to the west, we can see the larger mass of Richardson's Rock. Unseen beneath us is a pinnacle called Skyscraper. Farther west, closer to Richardson's, but also unseen, is the Boomerang pinnacle. All these pinnacles sit on the sea floor, which slopes out around the islands. Between the pinnacles and the island, the sea floor is about 150 feet deep. On the north side, the floor slopes rapidly down to about 350 feet and then plunges abruptly into the 1500-foot depths of the Santa Barbara Channel.

We are riding at anchor on Skyscraper, our line draped over the top of the pinnacle below us. We are a small fiberglass cork tethered to a 150-foot-tall mountain of rock, out beyond the protection of the islands and the continent, at the mercy of the entire mass of the Pacific Ocean. It is unusually calm today. Normally, the endless winds and currents that stream down from the northwest make this area a heaving, churning hell, inhospitable to sporting and leisure craft, navigable only by massive freighters and the indomitable California gray whales who migrate annually up and down the coast. But a week ago,

Hurricane John smashed its way north from the southeastern Pacific, along the length of the Baja Peninsula, before turning east and dissipating over the North American continent. Today, the swells generated by that storm are moving north through this region, running into and countering the northwestern swell, almost canceling it out. Strange to think that a hurricane a week ago, hundreds of miles away, is the cause of the calm we experience here today.

I zip up my fleece-lined windbreaker, pull the hood close around my head, wrap both hands around the warmth of my steaming cup of tea, and walk forward to size up the situation. I've dived Wilson's Rock and Richardson Rock on numerous occasions over the past 30-plus years and dived Boomerang once, about 15 years ago. I've even achieved one of the most sought-after prizes of California divers—the "triple crown" of diving, three of the San Miguel pinnacles on a single trip.

But I've never dived Skyscraper. I'm older now and definitely not as strong as I used to be. I don't take the risks I used to take. I check out the size of the swell—no problem there. I look down the anchor line, following its creamy-white length as it disappears into the depths. The visibility doesn't look great, maybe 30 feet, and the overcast means there won't be much light at depth, but still, it looks tolerable. I watch the surface of the water where the line enters, searching for the telltale V-shaped wake that indicates a current. None visible. I watch some floating specks of foam near the boat. They are slipping back along the length of the boat, but very slowly. That means almost no current.

"Okay," I say to Jon, "let's do it."

He smiles and nods his approval, and we walk back to the stern to begin our gearing-up ritual. One of our companions, Chris, has dived Skyscraper before, so I ask him how deep the pinnacle is. He says the top is at about 60 feet.

Then he adds with a grin, "But it goes down from there."

Rising willingly to the bait, I reply "Oh, you mean I'm supposed to go *deeper* than the top? Wow. I never would have thought of that. What a concept!"

Chris and Jon and the nearby crewmember all chuckle.

Another veteran diver, John, reminds us of his first rule of diving. "Never dive deeper than the bottom."

Still chuckling, we head for our gear.

For a scuba diver, gearing up is an important ritual not to be taken lightly. Our lives depend on being properly equipped with well-maintained gear to protect and support us in the alien environment of the ocean. Our neoprene wetsuits must fit comfortably, so they hold just enough water in a thin layer between the suit and our body to act as an extra layer of insulation between the cold sea and us. Neoprene booties, gloves, and hood also provide insulation. Fins with large blades give us the power to move ourselves through the water, even with close to 100 pounds of gear wrapped around us, even against mild currents. A mask seals a small amount of air around our eyes, protecting them from the stinging saltwater and allowing us to see clearly. Weight belts provide a counterbalance to the buoyancy of the wetsuits, enabling us to achieve the negative buoyancy needed to descend below the surface of the water. A BC serves as an adjustable air bladder to which we can add or subtract air, becoming in effect our own personal elevators.

Our tanks and regulators are the most important pieces of equipment, containing and delivering the air without which we cannot survive for more than a few, short breathless minutes beneath the surface of the sea. One of the hoses attached to the regulator ends in a small console with three gauges: a compass for navigation, a pressure gauge that indicates how much air is left in the tank, and a dive computer that keeps track of our depth and time and tells us how much time we have left till we hit the "no decompression limit." Staying down beyond that limit should only be done with careful advanced planning. The ascent from such a dive must be slow and staged properly to permit controlled release of dissolved nitrogen from the blood. Otherwise, the nitrogen forms bubbles that can lodge in the blood vessels or lungs or spinal column. This condition, sometimes called "the bends," can cause permanent paralysis or even death.

It takes 10 to 15 minutes to gear up, checking off each step mentally as we go and assisting each other with zippers, straps, and cross-checks.

At last we are ready. The boat's divemaster stands at the bow entry gate with his checklist, noting each diver who enters the water. Like gawky, oversized penguins, we shuffle awkwardly in our fins from the bench to the gate, each in turn stepping out into the air and falling, falling the 8- to 10-foot distance from the heaving deck to the swelling water.

Cold!

The frigid water seeps rapidly into my wetsuit, pouring down my back, my arms, working its way around my body, down into my legs. *Cold.* I inhale sharply, involuntarily. Then I bubble to the surface and swim toward the anchor line where I wait for Jon to join me. We give each other the OK sign, release the extra air from our BCs, and begin our descent down the anchor line.

The water is dark green and murky. I can see only about 25 feet ahead of me sighting down the line. Down we go. My body has warmed up the layer of water in my suit now, so I feel pretty comfortable, but as we reach the 40-foot mark, I start to feel the old familiar "ice cream headache" on my forehead that tells me we are passing through a thermocline and entering a colder layer of water. Being a bit of a masochist, I push the button on my computer display and check the temperature—a brisk and bracing 51° F.

I vow not to do that again and direct my attention back down the line. Dimly, I can see shapes and color variations in the green now. The pinnacle emerges and takes form as we get closer.

There are actually two points to the pinnacle, splitting at about 100 feet and rising side by side from there, with a sharp groove between them. The anchor chain is draped across the near pinnacle, drooping over the groove, and then disappearing up over the side of the far pinnacle. We drop down from the anchor line onto the face of the near pinnacle and descend to 97 feet, closing in on the rock face to begin our exploration. What greets us is an astonishing, living monument. There is not a single square inch of naked rock. Everything is covered with multiple layers of living things: scallops with their straight, broad, yellow lips open to the currents; barnacles with red and blue muscles rhythmically extending and contracting their feathery gills like fragile claws grasping nutrients from the water; yellow and red sponges spreading haphazardly across the rocky substrate; tiny feathery stalks of hydra sprouting from the sponges; three-foot tall stalks of golden-brown palm kelp accenting the landscape; and everywhere, colony after colony of inch-wide corynactis anemones, each colony a collection of clones of a uniform color, and every colony a different color. Lavender, pink, red, strawberry, peach, orange, blue—the variety of shades and colors is incredible. Each animal wears a circlet of white tentacles as a crown, so each colony looks like a bouquet of exotic flowers or a microcosmic display of holiday fireworks.

Sprinkled among the colorful colonies are the pure white stalks and fluffy powder-puff tops of the Metridium anemone. At this depth, they are relatively small, only three- to four- inches tall. But I can see, farther down the side of the pinnacle, several larger individuals, a foot or more tall.

We move slowly along the face of the near pinnacle. Occasionally, we spot a chestnut cowrie nestled among the mounds, its speckled mantle drawn partway up over its glossy cream-and-brown shell. And here is a large speckled sea lemon—a shell-less snail or nudibranch, bright yellow with black back, sporting white gills on its back like the plume of a circus pony.

We angle right and follow the anchor chain across the gap to the far pinnacle. I move in for a close-up look and spot the brilliant purple body and orange fringe of a Spanish shawl nudibranch, a small one, less than an inch long, nestled among the anemones and sponges. As I watch it sway with the gently moving water, Jon taps me on the shoulder and points to the right. A four-foot lingcod swims gracefully, lazily past us, heading nowhere in particular. Its massive head and flaring gill covers seem too large for its body, but both are mottled in the same pale sea-foam green with dark green and brown spots. I know from past experience that the flesh is that same pale green, as delicate and luminous as Chinese jade.

We work our way counterclockwise around the second pinnacle. Everything we see is alive, the rock crowded, glutted with living

A Living Rainbow   San Miguel Island, California
Photos Courtesy of Jon Fellows ©

creatures. Several large sheepshead swim near us, a huge male with his characteristic broad, red, vertical stripe covering his midsection and three or four large solid red females. The females are so big, I am amazed they haven't made the sex change to male yet. The only thing preventing that is the presence of the large male. This is a strong sign of a robust and healthy reef, and I feel a buoyancy of spirit that has nothing to do with how much air is in my BC.

Halfway around, we find another fish—a two-foot-long boccacio, sleek, speckled red and brown— swimming leisurely, not at all disturbed by our presence. We haven't seen any boccacio in years, let alone one this size. I watch it as it explores the nooks and crannies of the pinnacle and then disappears around the curve.

Now I've become aware of all the tiny stuff floating in the water around us, and I stop to focus on it. I had at first assumed that it was just sand and other inert particles suspended in the water column, but to my surprise, I see that each speck is a tiny fish, each less than a

½-inch long. There must be thousands, if not millions of them. They move in clouds, nervously darting into the reef face and then careening away in a swirling brown mass. Skyscraper is indeed a prolific nursery!

I pause to check my dive computer. Maximum depth so far is 97 feet, current depth 78 feet, elapsed time 12 minutes. The line of small dots climbing up the left side of the display gives me a graphic image of how much bottom time I have left. The dots extend two-thirds of the distance along the green curve. We're still comfortably within the no-decompression limit, but we will have to start our ascent before the line of dots reaches the end of the green curve.

We continue to fin slowly around the second pinnacle, floating effortlessly two to four feet out from the face of the reef, greedily taking in the profusion of color and form. We drift back across the gap and move in close to the first pinnacle, working our way slowly up toward the peak. I feel like a float in the Macy's parade, wafting in slow motion around the top of the Empire State Building. I hear carousel music in my head, and I feel as though I've just grabbed the brass ring. I flex my hands and they feel stiff from the cold, but I realize that I haven't spent even a second thinking about being cold.

I want to continue this ride for hours, spinning slowly in a dream around this incredible living rainbow. But alas, my computer tells me it's time to start our ascent. We've spent 18 enchanting minutes here, and I've gathered enough visual images and memories to last me a lifetime. Now we must return to the surface . . . and begin planning our next descent.

CHAPTER 5

LIQUID TIME TRAVEL

Paul

Ask people who have grown up or lived for an extended time near a coastline where they would like to live. Whether east coast, west coast, or any coast, it does not matter. Most will give you the same answer. They cannot exist far away from the ocean. I grew up on the East Coast, in New York. Judy grew up in the farm country of central Pennsylvania but spent her summer vacations at "The Shore." She did her first stint of graduate school in landlocked Indiana and fled to the California coast as soon as she was out of school and on her own. No offense to America's Heartland, but I don't think either of us could ever live in Kansas or Missouri.

The pull of the ocean seems almost a primal attraction for humans, an inbred genetic urge from our earliest ancestors beckoning us to return to our origins. Is it a coincidence that the salinity level of our blood is almost the same as saltwater, or that a human fetus has gill-like structures at its earliest stage of development? Perhaps, but there is no doubt that land mammals evolved from oceanic life-forms. We are truly creatures of the sea, although eons-evolved from Mother Ocean's womb.

Summers for me always meant walking a beach. Born in Brooklyn, but growing up in Manhattan until age 10, required taking the *Sea Beach*

Express or the *Brighton Beach Express* to the Coney Island section of Brooklyn. Those wonderful descriptive names, now converted to boring letters—the N and Q trains—evoked sun-drenched images of our final destination, even while the train sped through dark tunnels. We walked from the last stop of the elevated subway, *The El*, as we called it (Hmmm, is the term "elevated subway" an oxymoron?) and then proceeded across, or sometimes under, the boardwalk, which was like stepping through a magical passageway leading from the city's hard cement to the powdery, foot-searing sand and the cool, foamy surf beyond.

An even bigger annual thrill was summer vacation, visiting my cousins Bobby and Cathy in Freehold, New Jersey. Body surfing at Manasquan Beach, we faced towering breakers and fought ripping undertows. What a blast! Each day, speeding to and from the beach down country back roads in their white, 1953 Chevy (lots of chrome and hard, plastic interior without seat belts) was a thrill in itself. How did we ever survive our youth?

Moving to Bay Ridge, Brooklyn, when I was almost 11 meant "graduating" from the relatively calm Coney Island surf to the wild breakers of Riis Park in Queens, New York, with my three buddies, Steve, Larry, and Paul. As soon as we saw their dad's black-and-white 1956 Chevy Impala driving up the block on a sizzling summer afternoon, we'd jump off our stoops (Brooklyn has "blocks" and "stoops," the rest of the world has streets and front steps), change into swim trunks, and grab towels. Then we would hop into his car for a 30-minute ride along the Belt Parkway to Riis Park's fabulous white sand beach near the Rockaway section of Queens. That was where we "cut our teeth," and a few other body parts, learning to ride powerful waves that tossed us around and upside down like toothpicks, before slamming us onto the shell-strewn beach.

Years later in college, dating my future wife, Carol, entailed many fun-filled weekend summer afternoons at Riis Park. Since Carol and I were both beach lovers, we knew that we would instill an appreciation for ocean life in our children. Years later, watching our two little girls, Christine and Laura, walking ahead of us along the surf line, really opened my eyes to the almost supernatural hold the ocean has on children. They walked, skipped, and danced through the surf in a world of their own, occasionally stopping to pick up a rubbery sliver of jelly fish, examine a shiny black "mermaid's purse" (skate egg case), or dip a dull scallop shell into the salt water and watch Mother Ocean magically restore the shell's beautiful colors. A special treat was finding small red sea stars in shallow, rocky pools left by the last high tide. It was amusing to watch other children walking toward us, their eyes glued to the wet sand, holding a small pail and carefully picking up perfect shells as if they were collecting handfuls of treasure.

Now that our girls are grown and on their own, we hope they will pass along their love of the ocean to their children. As empty nesters, we're still beach lovers, enjoying Long Island's world-class Jones Beach. For me, that still means riding waves, a liquid time-transport system. The calendar tells me my chronological age. But Mother Ocean lets me feel the younger age of my heart and soul. All those years of body surfing in Brooklyn, New Jersey, and Queens have provided unforgettable lessons that come flooding back as soon as I arrive at a beach and the ocean engulfs my senses.

Arriving in the parking lot, you first smell the ocean, a salty, slightly fishy smell stronger at low tide, especially with an onshore breeze. Next, you hear the sound of breaking waves. A continuous, crashing roar promises an adventurous day riding the surf. Silence usually means a peaceful day, floating or just swimming parallel to shore. Walking across the sand, you finally see the waves, your first opportunity to "read" the ocean. Depending on the wind, movement of sand, and tides, the waves in the same location can look and act very differently from day-to-day. An ocean beach can appear calm and tranquil one day but feature strong surf with powerful rip currents that could sweep unwary swimmers out to sea on another day. Sharp, curling breakers that crash close to shore usually portend short tumbling rides, and you know you will return home battered and bruised after the waves have slammed you into the sand all day. Rolling breakers forming farther out promise longer rides, which will end at the shore-line after the wave's energy is spent.

Riding waves is a skill that, like bicycle riding, once learned is never lost. First, you wade into the cool surf and force your way through the incoming and outgoing foamy surge, until you reach chest-deep water. Next, squinting through sun glare reflecting off the surface, you watch approaching waves and pick out a promising swell far offshore. *This one looks good. No, too small. The one behind seems better.* You prepare, turn toward shore but glance over your shoulder as the wave you have chosen rises and starts to break. Next, curl your toes to gain purchase in the soft sand, so at the critical moment, you can push off for momentum, leaping forward, head down, arms extended. You will know in about three seconds if you timed your lunge right. If you mistimed it, your momentum immediately slows as the wave surges past, leaving you behind wallowing in its wake like an injured fish. But if you timed it correctly, the fun begins as the wave envelopes you and propels you toward shore.

Unlike a boogie boarder who rides on top of the crest, you become one within the wave. You feel its power lift you and then accelerate your prone body, entering the magic of liquid time travel. These days, I begin this ride as a 67-year-old baby boomer, but as the wave propels me forward in a surge of foamy bubbles, extended palms slicing through the water, time slips away. I become that 1960s teenager again, riding the waves many summers ago with my friends. I am exhilarated, lost in the roaring sound within the wave.

But all too soon, I'm jarred back to reality, as the belly I never had as a skinny teenager scrapes the sandy shore, prematurely terminating my ride back in time. Kneeling in the surf as the spent wave returns to the ocean, I glance around, gratified that I passed most of the other bodysurfers, many half my age. I turn and wade back toward deeper water, searching for the next wave, again and again and again.

CHAPTER 6

ENTER SPLASHING

Judy

Some 2,500 years ago, the wise old Chinese philosopher Lao Tzu said, "There are many paths to enlightenment." And just as there are many paths to enlightenment, there are many ways to enter the water to start your snorkeling or diving adventure. Most people think of scuba divers being well below the surface, exploring the ocean depths. But in order to do that, the divers have to get from here to there—and sometimes that can be a challenge! It can also be more fun than a barrel of sea monkeys. Of course, entry methods vary depending on whether you are entering from a boat or from the shore.

Boat Entries

During my introductory scuba class, my diving instructor taught us the classic method of entry called the Giant Stride. Of course, we must begin from the beginning, with the highly ritualized and elaborate "suiting up" ceremony. Don your bathing suit, then your wetsuit (or dive skin for tropical waters). Don't forget your booties, to keep your feet warm and blister-free, and your hood to keep your head warm. If you have long hair, the hood also prevents your hair from being converted into a massive, tangled saltwater-soaked wharf rat's nest. Spit in your mask (or if you're squeamish, use a commercial cleaning solution) to prevent fogging, and then rinse it well in ambient temperature saltwater. Check your tank to make sure it has a full air fill. Check your BC to be sure it is attached securely to the tank and adjusted properly for your body. Attach your regulator to the air valve, open the valve, and take a test breath from the regulator to ensure that it is working properly. Sling your weight belt into place.

Gather up your mask, gloves, and fins, and stash them on a bench conveniently located near the exit gate. If you are planning to take a speargun or a camera, stash that in the same location, or give it to one of the ever-helpful deckhands. Then get your tank, carry it gracefully across the pitching, heaving deck to the bench, where you sit to don the tank and buckle or otherwise fasten all the straps. Put some air into your BC so you will be buoyant when you enter the water. If you're overly cautious like me, you can again take a test breath from your regulator. Put on your mask and gloves, grab your fins, and hobble, again gracefully but also *carefully*, over to the gate.

With one hand holding the railing to steady yourself, put on your fins. At this point, you may either take your spear/camera from the deckhand or ask him/her to hand it to you after you enter the water. Put your snorkel (or regulator if you prefer) in your mouth, hold one hand over your mouth and mask, and then finally keeping your legs straight, thrust one leg forward out over the water. Push off with the foot that is still (hopefully) on deck and launch yourself like a giant pair of scissors out and down. As your feet hit the water, continue keeping your legs straight, but bring them forcefully together (like closing a pair of scissors). This movement will keep you from plunging too far below the surface. Also as you hit the water, exhale sharply to expel any water from your snorkel or regulator. The air in your BC will bring you bobbing to the surface, where you can gather your wits about you, again check that all straps are tightened and that your regulator is working, collect your spear/camera if needed, and—Voila!—you are finally ready for that dive.

I Demonstrate the Giant Stride Entry   Silver Bank Whale Sanctuary, Dominican Republic
Photo Courtesy of Christopher Guglielmo ©

Why do I suggest you hold one hand over your mouth and mask as you jump? With all that gear on your body, you will hit the water with the force of several tons of TNT—enough to knock your regulator (or snorkel) out of your mouth and push your mask up over your forehead, especially if you happen to have your head angled forward as you look down toward the water. I found that out the hard way when I did my first entry from a bow gate, which is about twice as high above the waterline as a side gate. A bow entry is a long way to fall and results in a whomping hard landing. I hadn't been diving long, and for this first bow entry, I forgot to hold on to my mask and regulator, with the result that my regulator went flying, my mask migrated to the top of my head, and I spluttered to the surface, gasping and more than a little flustered. Never forgot that little detail again!

If you have to wait on the surface for your buddy, it's usually worthwhile to switch from your regulator to your snorkel to conserve your air. Consequently, some divers (and my coauthor Paul can speak from personal experience here) are unpleasantly surprised when they descend and try to breathe underwater from their snorkel. *Glub, glub!* (Note from Paul: "Yes, more than once!") It's those pesky little details that'll get you every time.

Of course, if you are just snorkeling, you can skip the steps for preparing and donning your tank, and you may not need any weights either. However, freedivers usually carry some weight to counteract the buoyancy of the wetsuit and decrease the amount of effort required to kick down below the surface.

You've probably noticed that the Giant Stride is about as far removed from the techniques required for board diving as you can possibly get. In board diving, the goal is to minimize splash by narrowing and elongating the body (arms together over the head, legs straight and together with feet pointed), and the diver enters the water headfirst (really, arms first), slicing deep quickly. In contrast, water entries for scuba divers are designed to make as big a splash as possible and keep you from going too deep too fast—very similar to the goal of the "cannonball" entry (that favorite technique of teenage boys trying to impress teenage girls). Not to mention that it's extremely difficult to look sleek and graceful and in control while encased in a hundred pounds of bulky dive gear and stumbling around on a pitching boat deck. So if you want to look glamorous, take up board diving not scuba diving!

While the Giant Stride is still the most popular entry technique for diving from a standard dive boat, I have witnessed many variations and deviations from this over the years. Our good friend, Steve, who was an avid and accomplished photographer, preferred to sit on the rail with both arms wrapped around his camera, held close to his chest. With his regulator in his mouth, he would then push himself over backward and hit the water with his back, his arms and legs still curled protectively around that camera. Immediately after hitting the water, he would uncurl, rotate, orient, and head straight for the bottom.

Steve's technique was one I admired greatly but was never able to do myself. My ears have always been rather cranky and difficult to clear, so I am forced to descend slowly, preferably hanging onto the anchor line (or a handy strand of kelp) so I can pace my descent and clear my ears every few feet. Slow and not very elegant, but functional for those of us with pressure-challenged ears.

While most dive boats have gates that open the whole section of railing or sideboard so there is no obstruction, one of the boats we chartered had about a foot of sideboard that was not removable. It was necessary to step up onto the sideboard with one foot and swing the other foot up and over in order to enter the water. Fine. I could handle that, I thought, as I watched other divers doing it. But when I tried it, the boat viciously and deliberately lurched upward at precisely the right moment, so as I tried to swing my foot up and over, the sideboard hit the tip of my fin, causing me to lose my balance as my momentum carried me headfirst into the water. Again, I spluttered to the surface, this time with my mask hanging down around my neck. The offending fin had flipped off my foot and had landed on deck, forcing me to return to the boat and try again. This time, I was able to outwit the wily boat and made a successful entry. But I've never spoken to that boat again.

For well over two decades, Jon and I did most of our diving in Southern California with the Santa Monica Blue Fins, one of the finest collections of skilled, fun-loving, avid scuba divers I've ever known. Our members came from all walks of life and enriched our lives with their unique personalities and approaches to diving. I've introduced some of these delightful personalities in my book, *The Universe Next Door*. Now, I'd like to share the more unique and memorable entry techniques favored by them.

Kim, a solid, well-muscled force of nature whose passion for wreck diving (and brass) led him to enter the water with doubles (a pair of forty-pound tanks side by side) on his back for breathing and another set of doubles under his arm (to power his air hammer).

Paul and Vince prided themselves on being able to beat the anchor to the bottom. Vince, in fact, sat on the bow of the *Scuba Queen* fully suited-up for about four hours one day, as Skipper Pete roamed the ocean trying to find Cortez Banks, a reef structure about 90 miles off the coast. Although Pete was one of the best dead-reckoning skippers on the entire coast, he had apparently misplaced the reef sometime during our all-night journey. Fortunately, the Coast Guard was lurking near the reef on patrol. Apparently thinking we were poachers or other reprehensible seagoing criminals, they came roaring up to us, at which point Pete 'fessed up to them that he couldn't find Cortez, and the Coast Guard gallantly escorted us there. I don't think Pete ever got over the embarrassment, but Vince's patience was finally rewarded when we arrived at the reef.

And our Blue Fins were nothing if not inventive. When the first drysuits came out for sport divers, two of our members, Ron and Mike, were among the first to own them. These were Unisuits, made of the same neoprene as wetsuits, but with seals to prevent water from entering the suit. Unlike the roomier drysuits of today, which are designed to accommodate a set of "woolies" between the suit and the body, the Unisuit was designed to use a layer of air as its insulation. On our first evening of a multiday trip to the Northern Channel Islands, Ron and Mike proceeded to demonstrate the joy of drysuits for us. They both inflated their suits with the push-button air valve that connected the suit to the air tank. When they reached maximum inflation, they closely resembled twin floats in the Macy's Christmas Parade. They jumped overboard, landing with a loud double "splat," and then bobbed and rolled like a couple of crazed red beach balls as they chased each other around the boat. It made a great floor show for our evening cocktail hour as the crew prepared dinner for us.

Of course, boat entries have to be adapted to the nature of the boat. All the techniques I've described so far are designed for large hard-deck boats. But sometimes the large boat will carry small dinghies or inflatables to ferry divers from the main boat to various nearby dive spots. For these situations, the best entry technique is to suit up on the main boat and enter the dinghy carrying your mask, fins, and snorkel. Usually the crew will help you put your tank on as you sit on the side of the dinghy. You then just fall over backward, remembering to hold onto your mask and regulator. For these entries, it's important to straighten your legs as you fall, so your legs and fins don't hit the side of the dinghy.

In contrast, if you are using an inflatable as a base for snorkeling, you may want to utilize one of the most delightful entries I have ever learned: the Richie-Bounce, named for the divemaster who taught me the entry while we cruised the islands of Tonga on the diveboat *Nai'a*. To do the Richie-Bounce, don your mask, snorkel, and fins, stand near the side of the boat and jump, flexing your knees and hips so your shins bounce off the top of the inflatable's side. As your shins hit, use the flexibility of the inflatable and push with your lower legs to send you cartwheeling, heels-over-head, so you land in the water on your back. Note: do not try this in an aluminum or wooden dinghy!

You can view the Richie-Bounce here:
http://tinyurl.com/The-Richie-Bounce

Another very functional entry for snorkeling, from either a dinghy or inflatable, is the "slither." This entry is useful if you are whale watching and want to get into the water without alarming the whales. Put on your mask, snorkel, and fins in the boat, and then slowly and quietly slip over the side of the boat headfirst, holding on to the side to slow your entry and minimize the amount of splashing as you enter. The slither is easier from an inflatable but can be done from a dinghy also.

Shore Entries

Shore entries are typically more challenging that boat entries. To begin with, you must choose and port all your gear to the target beach. Some beaches are easier to get to than others. For example, in Southern California, there are a number of beaches that can only be reached by hiking down a steep trail or a long flight of stairs. Usually, such

locations have names like "Heart Attack Hill" and other equally colorful and inspiring monikers.

Once you get there, you do your suiting-up routine on the beach,
preferably without getting tons of sand in your wetsuit or mask or regulator. Then you must make your way into the water and through the
surf, usually followed by a long swim out to the destination reef. For
myself, I find all this way too much work and bother, so I mostly stick
to boat diving. But for those of you who are game enough, the first
thing you'll want to learn is that waves come in sets, with a series of
smaller waves being followed by a series of larger waves. You'll want
to sit on the beach for a while and watch the waves to determine how
many waves are in each set, and then time your entry to coincide with
the smaller waves of the set. You'll also want to identify any areas where
waves "bend" or two side-by-side waves come in at different angles,
resulting in turbulence in the "V" where they meet. These conditions
usually result in riptides, which you will definitely want to avoid!
There may also be large boulders hidden under the waves. These cause
the type of turbulence known as "boilers," also something you want to
avoid. And finally, you'll want to identify where the reef is relative to
your entry point, and set a compass course, so you'll be able to find it
even if the visibility is poor (which it frequently is near shore).

Having timed the wave sets, identified riptides and boilers, and set
your compass course, you then need to choose which of two methods
of getting through the surf you want to employ. The first method is
to put everything on except your fins, then walk into the water facing
the waves. Once you reach waist-high water (inside the zone where
the waves break), you can don your fins and begin swimming into
the waves. The second method is to put on your fins first, and then
walk backward into the water. This makes it easier to put your fins on,
but more difficult to watch the waves, since you have to keep looking
over your shoulder (and yes, they probably *will* be gaining on you).
Additionally, if the surf is fairly strong, the outward flow of the water,
which travels along the bottom, can actually push under your fins
and lift you off the bottom, making it extremely difficult to keep your

balance. Of course, if there is little (or no) wave action, either method will work, but then, where's the challenge in *that*?

If it's true challenge you want, I highly recommend doing a rocky entry. As with the beach entry, it is necessary to spend time watching the waves and timing the sets. But here, you'll probably want to time your entry to coincide with the biggest waves in the set. Work your way out onto the rocks until you are in the zone where the biggest waves hit, put on your fins, and then push out into a large wave as it starts to retreat. You'll need to kick strongly to power yourself out through the waves to avoid getting thrown back onto the rocks. Bourbon on the rocks is good—diver on the rocks, not so much.

And Exit Laughing

Of course, for every entry, you will most likely want to do an exit. (This is one of those situations in which symmetry is highly desirable.) Before I began diving, I had visions of being Ursula Andress as Honey Ryder in that classic James Bond movie, *Dr. No*, emerging from the sea with water dripping in seductive rivulets down my long limbs, as I inspected my sea treasures and nonchalantly hummed, "Underneath the Mango Tree." And of course, my coauthor confesses that as an avid teenage Bondophile, the flip side of that same scene is forever seared in his male brain, with himself as Bond greeting Honey as she emerged from the water. Sadly, it's not usually like that, for any of us divers, male or female.

Getting back on board a charter dive boat that is being tossed about by large rolling swells and wind-driven chop is no stroll on the beach. You have to time your exit so that you lunge for the swim platform at the back of the boat as it dips low into the water and then hold on for dear life as the swell brings the entire platform up out of the water, only to have it crash back down again as you are trying desperately to get your fins off and your feet under you.

On the brighter side, some of my diving friends have demonstrated great style in their boat exits, for example by ascending the ladder from the swim step draped with casual elegance in great swathes of giant kelp, the leaves glistening like a movie starlet's fabulous golden feather boa. Others have emerged bedecked in hundreds of tiny living krill-like animated red sequins. Some divers storm the swim step and ladder like conquering heroes, brandishing their game bags heavily laden with the day's kill, whether fish or shellfish, for all to see. But my personal favorite will always be my good friend Molly who stepped nonchalantly onto the deck after her dive, removing her tank and BC to reveal three respectable-sized abalone stuck tenaciously to her wet-suit. She had neglected to take her game bag with her but managed to persuade her prey to attach themselves to her, just as they usually attach themselves to their home rocks! A brilliant adaptation on the part of the diver but certainly maladaptive for the hapless abalone.

As for reboarding a dinghy or inflatable, such exits frequently are quite challenging, even in calm waters, especially if the vessel doesn't have a ladder that can be lowered. Sometimes you can use the rhythm of the swells to give you a lift as you hold onto the side of the boat (or the ropes on the inflatable). If you can get your body high enough so you can bend at the waist, you can then usually grab something inside the boat so you can swing your legs over and into. Alternatively, I have had a crew member reach over so we could lock forearms together, and then he would levitate me up and over and into the boat. Once, I was lifted so forcefully that I almost went flying all the way across and back into the water on the other side of the boat! In any case, I always feel more like a beached whale than like Ursula Andress. (*Sigh.*)

And speaking of beaches, exits there are usually pretty easy if you time them to coincide with the wave sets. The motion of the waves carries you into the shore with little effort, but then there's that minor detail of trying to stand up in the middle of crashing surf and remove your fins before the next wave hits. And the last time I tried a rocky exit, I got slammed into the rocks by the powerful churning surf and had one of my fins stripped off and carried away. Of course, that made it easier to get my fins off quickly, since I now had only one to worry about, and then I made a mad scramble for the drier rocks farther in, where I could finally stand up and act nonchalant for the benefit of the non-divers watching us from the beach. I even hummed a few bars of "Underneath the Mango Tree" as I casually picked my way across the remaining rocks to the smooth sandy beach, with water dripping in seductive rivulets down my wetsuit from the seaweed draped in clotted clumps across my shoulders.

CHAPTER 7

BARRACUDAS I HAVE MET

Paul

Hanging with Elvis and Hercules

Barracuda. Say the name out loud and slowly. It conjures up images of predation, stealth, fierceness, and dominance. The name commands respect and makes you pay attention. Perhaps that's why one U.S. car manufacturer, Plymouth, named one of its models the *Barracuda*. Think about it. Naming a car after a fish? You wouldn't be caught dead driving a *Tuna*, right? But a *Barracuda*! Now *that* makes people sit up and take notice.

An entertaining pirate flick that occasionally appears on late-night television is *The Spanish Main*, a 1945 classic, starring Maureen O'Hara as the lovely Contessa Francesca. The evil Viceroy of Cartagena, played by Walter Slezak, kidnaps the Contessa from her lover, the hero pirate, known as The Barracuda, played by Paul Henreid (Humphrey Bogart's costar in *Casablanca*). His pirate vessel is also called *The Barracuda*. During the movie's confrontational encounter, Slezak called his nemesis by his pirate name, his lines slowly dripping off his tongue like cold syrup. "So, you are the *Barra-coo-da!*" Of course, The Barracuda eventually prevailed.

I once read a 1970s *Reader's Digest* article about barracudas. The point of the story was that barracudas were mean, dangerous fish and the true cause of many attacks falsely attributed to sharks. One account mentioned a fisherman who leaned over the side of his boat as he wrestled a hooked marlin aboard. A large barracuda suddenly leaped from the water and ripped a fist-sized chunk of flesh from the unfortunate angler's neck. *Ouch!*

It was against this mental backdrop that I experienced my first close barracuda encounter. Carol and I were snorkeling at the Club Med reef in Cancun. The water was crystal clear; the coral reef was amazingly beautiful and hosted a wide variety of fish. We were in water only about 10 feet deep, when a huge barracuda, easily five feet long, languidly swam under us, hugging the bottom. I froze for several seconds, hoping not to attract the beast's attention. Then I looked up to warn Carol, but she was nowhere to be found. I noticed a pair of thrashing fins about 20 yards ahead of me, paddling rapidly toward shore. "Hey, there's a barracuda here!" I shouted to my wife, protectively concerned for her welfare. She looked back at me over her shoulder, through her wake.

"I know. I saw it coming. Didn't you?" she replied.

"No!"

"I tried to warn you."

"Really? I didn't hear you," I replied dubiously, as I energetically began thrashing my own fins to catch up.

Finally we reached shore. Breathless, I told one of the staff, "Hey, there a giant barracuda right out there!"

"Was it a real big one?" he inquired."

"Yeah, real big!"

"Swimming very slowly along the bottom?"

"Yeah, I guess so."

"Oh, that's just Elvis. He comes by a lot."

"Oh," I said. "You mean that monster has a name? *Elvis*?"

The Club Med staff member laughed. "Yes, that's what we call him. But don't worry. Even though we are an 'all-inclusive' resort, Elvis knows the guests are not allowed on his menu."

I smiled back, wondering if Elvis had read the fine print. We kept looking for him whenever we snorkeled but never saw him again.

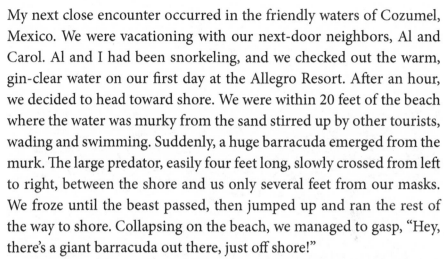

My next close encounter occurred in the friendly waters of Cozumel, Mexico. We were vacationing with our next-door neighbors, Al and Carol. Al and I had been snorkeling, and we checked out the warm, gin-clear water on our first day at the Allegro Resort. After an hour, we decided to head toward shore. We were within 20 feet of the beach where the water was murky from the sand stirred up by other tourists, wading and swimming. Suddenly, a huge barracuda emerged from the murk. The large predator, easily four feet long, slowly crossed from left to right, between the shore and us only several feet from our masks. We froze until the beast passed, then jumped up and ran the rest of the way to shore. Collapsing on the beach, we managed to gasp, "Hey, there's a giant barracuda out there, just off shore!"

One of the hotel employees arranging lounge chairs on the beach looked up. "Oh, you must have seen Hercules. He comes around all the time."

Elvis? *Hercules*? Do you sense a pattern here? Clearly these are fish with attitude, the neighborhood bullies full of bluster and bluff and perhaps bite, too!

We saw Hercules frequently the remainder of the week, usually in the vicinity of a large school of tiny silversides that he would herd just off the beach. Whenever he wanted a snack, he would dart into the school and emerge from the other side, licking his toothy chops while a glittering mass of scales drifted slowly to the bottom. Hercules usually ignored us, except when he thought our intent was to hijack his swimming buffet. Then he would charge us with an impressive threat display featuring snapping teeth.

Worldwide, there are about 20 species of barracudas. The species snorkelers and divers most frequently encounter in the Caribbean is *Sphyraena barracuda*, otherwise known as the great barracuda. They are impressive fish, befitting their name. Mature adults reach between four and six feet, and as they age, they grow robust, filling out the streamlined shape of their youth. They are armed with needle-sharp teeth, designed to slice smaller fish in half or rip hunks of flesh from larger prey. Their fierce reputation is enhanced by the fact that they tend to swim with their mouths slightly agape, as if intentionally showing off their dental ware.

The Great Barracuda   Cozumel, Mexico
Paul Mila Photo ©

These large barracudas are generally old and territorial. They stake out a prime location with plenty of food and no competitors. Some take up residence on a reef or occasionally near shore if there is a good food supply. There they live out their lives in the lap of fish luxury, until a slightly younger and stronger rival displaces them. Then, I suppose they swim off to barracuda heaven, where an unlimited supply of tiny delicious fish swims around them for eternity.

When scuba diving, I've seen barracuda countless times and while I still respect them, I feel very little fear. Swimming underwater with them, you feel less vulnerable than snorkeling on the surface like chum. Of course, this safe feeling is merely illusory, definitely a case of misplaced confidence. Barracudas are supreme sprinters, among the fastest fish in the sea, and can accelerate in the blink of an eye. If a 'cuda decided to attack a swimmer, snorkeler, or diver, there would be no escape. It would be all over in a split second. But the good news for divers is that most undersea close encounters are the result of barracudas' curiosity rather than aggression. They rarely attack, unless they are cornered or feel threatened.

I've crossed paths with juveniles swimming in twos and threes, or sometimes in packs of ten, curiously checking me out but with no apparent ill intent. Then, as you swim along the bottom of a reef you turn a corner and come face-to-face with a big ol' boy, under a coral outcropping in ambush mode, waiting for an easy meal. Nature has provided them with effective natural camouflage. Their underside is pale silver, so barracudas above you blend in with the bright surface.

An Impressive Old-Timer in Antigua
Paul Mila Photo ©

Their dorsal area is a darker blend of black stripes and irregular patterns, so when below you, they disappear into the reef background. The old-timers are especially impressive, with a middle-aged spread, giving them a massive, powerful appearance. Primarily, these are the barracuda divers are fortunate to see, while most fishermen and land-lubbers rarely do. These fish have survived to old age because they've been too smart to bite a baited hook.

The Big Boy of Palancar Reef

I had the pleasure of a surprise encounter with one of these giants one morning, diving Palancar Reef in Cozumel. Our multilevel dive plan called for a descent to 80 feet, where we would explore the deep part of the reef. Then, we would ascend to 40 feet and continue the dive until we were low on air. I had reached 80 feet and was comfortably observing the various corals and sponges.

I almost swam past, but a silvery glint caught my eye. I turned my head and saw him 10 feet below me, resting near the bottom against a coral wall, just hanging out, sleeping, or whatever a barracuda does

The Big Boy of Palancar Reef   Cozumel, Mexico
Paul Mila Photo ©

before noon. I slowly descended to his level, kicked my fins once, and let my momentum carry me toward him. He watched me but never moved as I glided closer, six feet, five, four, then finally halted at about three feet.

He was a beautiful fish, scales shimmering in the light penetrating the depths through the crystal-clear water. He was very large, almost five feet, and too thick to put your hands around, should you have the insane idea to try. He rotated an eye and looked at me in a way that I knew he was telling me this was *his* reef and I was merely an interloper. I slowly raised my Sea and Sea MX10, fitted with a strobe and 20-millimeter wide-angle lens for photographing large animals close-up. He twitched and opened and closed his mouth, body language advising me, *Okay, buddy, don't wear out your welcome!* I took the hint, pressed the shutter, and watched for any reaction to the flash.

Thankfully there was none, but he worked his jaws wider and faster, his needle-sharp dentures protruded from his mouth, and he twitched more noticeably. Clearly, he was losing patience, so I backed off.

See ya big fella, I said, departing the area, looking over my shoulder to make sure he did not decide to stalk me.

The Attack of the Death Express

A more recent barracuda encounter in Cozumel, Mexico, has made me rethink my slide into complacency regarding barracudas. As I mentioned earlier, the great barracuda is documented as one of the fastest predators in the sea. You can observe them as they hover almost motionless one second, and then speed off in attack mode in the blink of an eye. I had heard and read about their legendary speed and violence but had never witnessed it firsthand until one particular dive in Cozumel.

Our dive group spent our second dive of a two-tank dive on Paso de Cedral, a shallow reef, about 50 to 60 feet deep. We noticed a commotion near a coral head and swam over to investigate. We observed the local residents savagely attacking a yellow-tailed snapper. Queen triggers, mutton snappers, black durgons, and other yellow-tail snappers ripped chunks of flesh from the wounded fish and shredded its fins. At one point, the harried fish swam into a small cave to escape

Rushing in for the Kill   Cozumel, Mexico
Photo Courtesy of Dick Stuart ©

its tormentors. Captivated by the scene, we watched the queen triggers follow their victim into the cave and pull it out to continue their
relentless attack. Dive buddy Jeff Rein and I had our SeaLife cameras
on video mode, capturing the unfolding action.

We were so transfixed watching the action in our viewfinders
that we were oblivious to our surroundings. This snapper had been
eaten down to the bone—literally. But somehow, the attacking fish
had missed all the vital organs. We could see its exposed spine while
it continually zig-zagged and swerved, vainly swimming for its life.
Suddenly all the other fish scattered, and the wounded snapper turned
sharply, as if evading something.

The fish saw the danger that we did not. Two barracudas were bar-
reling in from the blue at high speed, like Amtrak's silver Acela express
trains. Both Jeff and I were so focused photographing the struggling snapper that we never noticed the Death Express as it rushed in for the kill.

The first barracuda, a silver-gray blur sped through the frame like
a runaway torpedo. It zoomed past our lenses so fast we didn't even

Attack of the Death Express   Cozumel, Mexico
Photo Courtesy of Dick Stuart ©

notice it until later, when we watched slow-motion replay. That 'cuda
missed the desperately swerving snapper, but his buddy's aim was
better! The second silver bullet hit the snapper with brutal violence,
seizing its victim crossways with its razor-sharp teeth inches below my
fins. I was just in front of Jeff, so he caught me in his video kicking away
the chomping barracuda with my yellow and black fins. With several
violent shakes, the barracuda sliced its victim in half. Diver Dick Stuart
captured the action with the two amazing photos above.

Were these two predators hunting cooperatively, like a fighter pilot
and his wingman, or competitively? My vote is they were competing
for their prize, as in, *May the best fish win.*

Mesmerized, I watched the remaining half of the snapper floating
lifelessly in a puff of misty-green blood. (At that depth, the color red
appears green.) Seconds later, a third barracuda whizzed past my head
from behind, just over my left shoulder. With a single bite, it devoured

the remainder of the half-eaten fish. Several more barracuda soon appeared out of the blue gloom, eager for an easy meal. We huddled together while they circled us menacingly.

You can view the attack on YouTube at:
http://tinyurl.com/barracuda-attack

During the attack, we felt like the settlers in a wild-west movie, huddling together for protection while the Indians surrounded our wagon train. I watched another barracuda rush Jeff as he continued shooting video. Jeff waved his arm as if swatting away a fly, and the aggressive fish veered off at the last second. Another one made a half-hearted charge at Alison and novice-diver Sylvia. Alison grabbed Sylvia and pulled her away from the area as several more barracuda arrived on the scene. Now we watched about six circling us. We felt relieved when the 'cudas left the area, several minutes later.

Back aboard our boat, we hooted and howled with excitement. We told Sylvia she might never experience a more exciting dive no matter how long she continues to dive. Alison informed us that diving more than 15 years in Cozumel, and logging thousands of dives, she had never before witnessed such a spectacle. Evidently the folks at National Geographic also thought the encounter was unique. They saw the video on Youtube and contacted me for an interview. They used the video on their *Caught in the Act* television show. Nat Geo even dubbed the episode *Zombie Fish*, in honor of the resilient, half-eaten yellow tail snapper that refused to die.

CHAPTER 8

SPRING BREAK LEVIATHAN-STYLE

Judy

Boring. Very boring. And frustrating.

It is Sunday, February 9, 2006, the first day of our five-day trip to Silver Bank aboard the charter dive boat *Turks & Caicos Aggressor II*, aka *TCA-II*. We are not here to dive but rather to observe and hopefully swim with humpback whales. We've spent over three hours this afternoon, bobbing around on a choppy ocean in our bright orange rubber ducky of an inflatable skiff (boldly named *Predator*) with very little to show for it. The heat of the sun has already negated the cooling effects of our swim a half hour ago, and my tropical wetsuit is once again becoming uncomfortably hot.

Skipper Piers stands patiently at the wheel and scans the horizon, aiming the boat first in this direction, then in that direction in his search for whales. The ultra-quiet low-emission four-stroke outboard motor hums and purrs unobtrusively. Lucie, the professional videographer on the crew, has her new high-definition digital video camera primed and ready. But the whales are simply not cooperating. So we sit and we bob and we wait.

Boring. Very boring.

There is absolutely no land visible here, only ocean from horizon to horizon, punctuated by our mother ship and the rusting old hulk of the wreck *Polyxeni*—a somber warning for any ship that dares to travel here. A young Dominican Republic couple talk quietly together while their daughters, 12-year-old Ysabella and 10-year-old Adriana, bounce up and down on the bow, hang over the side, and fidget, bored to distraction. Adriana loves the ocean and she is fairly patient, at least for a typical 10-year-old, but Ysabella doesn't care all that much and has had enough.

She wants some action, so she asks Piers, "Will the whales hear me if I do this?" and she shouts. Instantly, just behind her and about 20 feet away, an adult humpback whale breaches directly toward us, hurling its 30-foot-long, 30-ton body ¾ of its length out of the water, arching sideways and falling back into the water broadside, creating a gargantuan explosion of water and spray.

We explode, too! Whooping and laughing, we fumble for our cameras, suddenly wide awake and juiced on our own adrenaline. We were certainly not expecting such a spectacular show, and the look on Ysabella's face is a comical amalgam of shock, incredulity, and dawning delight at her apparent power. Forget about horse-whisperers and dog-whisperers—they have just been irrevocably and emphatically upstaged by the humpback-shouter.

To witness an adult humpback breaching up close and at sea level, as we just had, is more than sufficient to blow anyone's mind and leave you gasping and begging for more. Now *this* is what we had traveled so many thousands of miles to see!

The whales, too, had traveled thousands of miles to reach this place. After feeding all summer in the rich northern seas, they do not eat from the time they reach the West Indies until their return journey north the following summer. So why, you may ask, do these animals travel so far and starve themselves for five or six months? In a word: sex. Silver Bank is their breeding ground, their birthing place, and their nursery. A single adult humpback is 30–40 feet long and weighs 30–40 tons (1 ton per foot). That weight is roughly the equivalent of 10 elephants stuffed into a body the size of a school bus. Imagine roughly 3,000 such creatures cavorting in a single large area. Think Ft. Lauderdale during spring break or New Orleans during Mardi Gras, except that instead of thousands of hormone-crazed teenagers, you are dealing with thousands of 35-ton animated (and, yes, hormone-crazed) school buses. This is Spring Break Leviathan-Style!

Humpback vs. School Bus

- Length 30-40 feet
- Width 10-12 feet
- Weight 30-40 tons
- Pectoral 12-15 feet
- Max speed 3 knots
- Max passengers 1 calf

- Length 30-40 feet
- Width 8-9 feet
- Weight 5 tons
- Pectoral - none
- Max speed 65 mph
- Max passengers 84 kids

Judith Hemenway PowerPoint Illustration ©

The adult males arrive in the breeding area first, followed by the females. Some of the females are pregnant, having been impregnated the previous breeding season. They will give birth, typically to a single calf, though rarely twins are born.

While the new mothers with their babies are going about the serious business of ensuring the safety and health of the new generation, the other adult whales are having a grand and glorious party. The males strut their stuff by engaging in a variety of courting behaviors, hoping to impress the females with their strength, endurance, and prowess. These behaviors include tail slaps, tail lobs, pec slaps, breaches, and of course the long, complex songs for which humpbacks are famous.

Whale watching at Silver Bank is a deceptively simple business. Every morning after breakfast, all 17 of us passengers don our swimsuits and tropical wetsuits, grab hats, sunglasses, mask and snorkel, fins, and (most importantly) cameras, and pile into the 2 inflatable dinghies, *Conqueror* (with Skipper Piers at the helm) and *Predator* (with Second Skipper Christopher), and head out away from the *TCA-II* in search of whales. We spend the entire morning in the dinghies, returning to the *TCA-II* for lunch, and then dispersing again in the dinghies for the entire afternoon.

Sounds easy, doesn't it? Just sit in a boat in tropical waters for hours while someone else does all the driving. But in some ways, whale watching is physically more tiring than scuba diving. Diving has a steady rhythm: one hour down, then two hours rest on the main boat, relaxing in the comfort of the salon. In contrast, whale watching is much less predictable.

We spend three to four hours on the skiffs, bouncing and slapping around as the sun beats down on us from above and glares up at us in reflections off the water. We cannot predict when we will see whales, so there is no rhythm to speak of, and if we do find whales and have the opportunity to stay with them, that takes precedence over any scheduled meals. We may not have lunch until midafternoon or dinner as late as eight, by which time we are all exhausted and thoroughly sun-fried. But the opportunity to observe these magnificent mammals up close, in their own world, and on their terms is well worth all the sunburns, bruises, seasickness, and delayed dining.

During the five days we spend on the water at Silver Bank, we have dozens of close encounters with the whales, observing their surface behaviors from the dinghies and the *TCA-II*, and frequently having the opportunity to get in the water with them. No diving is permitted at Silver Bank, but it also is not necessary. The visibility of the water is usually good, and we are able, in many cases, to get close to the whales.

Even when the visibility is not exceptional, it is still relatively easy to spot these animals from the surface. Many ocean-dwelling fish and mammals, including humpbacks, have counter-shading (a dark dorsal surface and a light ventral surface), which is very effective as a camouflage. However, with the Atlantic humpbacks, not only is the bottom of their pectorals white, so is the top. It is these great white "wings" that enable us to spot them easily, even in murky waters. Chillingly, it is this characteristic that came to be branded "the hunter's mark" by the whalers, whose harpooners used that characteristic to zero in on their intended prey.

A Baby Showing Its "Hunters' Mark" White Pectorals   Silver Bank Whale Sanctuary, Dominican Republic
Judith Hemenway Photo ©

Monday, Day 2

Here we are in our little rubber ducky on Day 2, cruising the intense blue waters of Silver Bank in hopes of encountering the great white-winged whales. This is a very productive morning in terms of sur-face observations but no in-water time. For the first hour our group, aboard *Predator*, shadows a pair of sleepers. They rise and breathe 2 or 3 times, then go down for 15 to 20 minutes. They breathe consciously; they do not have autonomic regulation like we do. Consequently, only half their brain can sleep at any given moment; the other half must be awake to control their breathing.

For the second hour, we move near *Conqueror* and watch a trio—a mother, calf, and male escort. The male is doing repeated, fabulous pec slaps. Over and over again, in slow motion, he rolls on his side, raising his 15-foot long pec and slapping it forcefully on the surface to create an impressive spray and an emphatic *whomp*! The baby is quite active also, doing breaches and pec slaps, but his little pecs are very floppy.

For the third hour, we move away from *Conqueror* and find three courting pairs. One male does an impressive tail lob, sloshing the surface like a gigantic Mixmaster, and then he does a fine breach, propelling his body three-quarters of the way out of the water. With each move, we all whoop and shout, quite involuntarily and unabashedly, as we frantically snap photos in our attempts to capture these gargantuan beasts in our puny cameras.

Tuesday, Day 3

A fabulous morning! We're with Christopher in *Conqueror* and at first, see nothing. But then we find a mother and baby with a young male escort and spend an hour and a half with them. Mom and Baby are both easygoing and relaxed and Baby is playful, practicing tail slaps and pec slaps with her floppy little flukes and pecs. She rolls and slides over Mom's rostrum, loping along just above Mom, which is called slipstreaming. She even does a couple of little breaches and pokes her head up out of the water in a spyhop or two.

But the male escort is obnoxious. He keeps himself between us and the mother and baby, and as soon as we get in the water, he herds them away from us. Of course, that's excellent survival behavior for the whales but frustrating for us human looky-loos. I do get a good look at him once when I get in, and he stays still long enough that I'm able to get fairly close to Mom and Baby. The escort (I call him Little Ahnold) is directly below me at 15 to 20 feet; I'm just above his tail. The visibility is milky, but I can see Mom about 25 feet away near the surface with Baby cavorting above her. But then I see Little Ahnold move his tail (ever so slowly and slightly) and curve off to the right to herd them away from us—and they're gone.

It's remarkable how fast they can move with very little apparent effort—no emphatic tail swishes or body flexing, just a barely perceptible tail movement or a slow, casual drawing of pecs close to the body.

Suddenly you realize that even if you had an outboard motor in place of your fins, you couldn't keep up with them.

We follow them for another hour, but Little Ahnold is determined to keep us away. We give up and look elsewhere for other action. That leads us to Piers and *Predator* and a huge male doing repeated pec slaps to try to impress his female companion. His pecs are easily 15 feet long. What's remarkable about him is an enormous gash just in front of his dorsal fin, a cut maybe two to three feet wide all the way down through the blubber and extending three feet down on both sides. The chunk of blubber is still attached on one side, flopping back and forth as he moves. It has the look of a propeller cut, absolutely horrible, but appears to be healing. It

A Large Male Does Repeated Pec Slaps as We Observe   Silver Bank Whale Sanctuary, Dominican Republic
Photo Courtesy of Jon Fellows ©

certainly doesn't slow him down. He just keeps slapping those pecs over and over again. Sometimes, he has both pecs up in the air simultaneously (at which point he is rolled over belly-up). After a half hour, the female disappears but the male (we've dubbed him Chunky Monkey) continues to slap, finally settling down about a half-hour later. We don't try to get in the water but stay on *Conqueror* and observe from there, our cameras clicking repeatedly.

After lunch, we get our first look at a rowdy bunch, which is common breeding season group behavior. There are several groups of whales, with two or three whales in each group, and all are doing power swims, which are apparently the humpback whale version of wind sprints. The groups do not directly interact with each other, and the direction of their movements is random, so they're not racing against each other. They seem to be using their power swims to demonstrate their strength and speed (and perhaps their buddy-bonding) to the other groups.

Another behavior, very similar to power swimming, is the freight train. For this, the whales line up in a single line (approximately) and swim hell-bent-for-blubber, ranging far and wide over the expanse of the Silver Bank. This is an awe-inspiring sight, and the term freight train doesn't convey the full psychic impact of the behavior. Imagine a freight train composed of a line of sentient steam locomotives, all fully charged, huffing and puffing huge volumes of steam, and barely able to confine their forward movement to a myriad of railroad tracks that branch out across the vast expanse of the Great Plains. If your imagination is vivid enough, you may begin to appreciate the incredible power of a humpback train.

In between the more exciting encounters with the whales, we bounce and bob for many hours in our little rubber duckies as we watch for more whales. We use this time to check our camera gear, chat with our fellow passengers, take a little siesta, and garner knowledge of the humpbacks from the skippers and crew.

During one long, uneventful interlude, when all we are seeing is a few breaches far off on the horizon, Christopher informs us, in all seriousness, that there are actually two species of whales on the Bank: the well-known humpbacks and the lesser-known horizon whales.

During those hours when only the horizon whales are active, both Piers and Christopher regale us with a large collection of their own whale tales, including these:

❖ Numerous instances in which male escorts have slapped the dinghies with either a tail or a pectoral fin, behavior that clearly was intended to warn the dinghies to keep their distance. In every instance, these slaps had been gentle with no intent to harm.

❖ One instance in which an amorous female came up directly under Christopher's dinghy, her belly facing up. She lifted both her pecs out of the water on either side of the boat and gave it a giant hug before gently releasing it and dropping away.

❖ An overeager and socially insensitive photographer, who repeatedly pursued a mother and baby too closely and too aggressively. He ignored the crew's advice to back off and be more careful until finally the escort whale swam up to him and whacked his leg with one pectoral fin, slashing the leg open. No surgery was required, but the wound did require lots of antibiotics and bandages.

❖ The Great Silver Bank Sleigh Ride. *Predator*, with Piers at the helm, had found a group of humpbacks, mother and baby in the middle, flanked on each side by three males who herded her around pretty brutally. Piers called it "gang rape." The baby rode on his mother's rostrum, and Piers said they could hear the little guy crying and squealing. The males were trying to mate with the mother, and things got pretty out of hand. That was when the skiff got lifted onto the back of one whale, and then slid over onto the back of another. They finally slid off and out of the action with no harm done.

Wednesday, Day 4

A half-hour out, we find three males duking it out over a female. Two are fairly small males, probably 30 to 32 feet/tons each, but Bruiser (as I have named him) is "easily thirty-eight tons," says Piers.

Bruiser has incredible power and attitude. He sticks his head out of the water as he swims, revealing the rows of tubercles that bristle across his rostrum. He thrusts his big bulb of a chin forward, breathes heavy and hard, and snorts emphatically. With each breath his blow-hole opens and closes vigorously. He also executes sharp, angular power dives. No flukes show on those dives, but we can see the muscles in his huge back ripple and surge as he slices downward.

Another of his favorite actions is to come to the surface and grab a huge mouthful of air (expanding his rorqual pleats to hold as much air as possible), then dive down and blow long bubble curtains as he swims.

And of course, we jump into the water right in the middle of it all. At one point, I look down as one of the smaller males dives at an angle from my right across and in front of me, maybe 30 feet down and 30 feet ahead. Seconds later, Bruiser dives down from my left, aiming straight for the head of the smaller male. It looks like Bruiser hits/pushes him, and then they both rise to the surface in front of me. A little later, I watch one male surface in front of and head away from me. I lift my head out of the water in time to see him do a powerful tail lob about 50 feet in

Bruiser Bashes Past Me   Silver Bank Whale Sanctuary, Dominican Republic
Photo Courtesy of Lori Fulton ©

front of me. All this time, the female leisurely hangs out below along the sidelines, letting the guys do their thing. The power and intensity of these animals are stunning, remarkable, and awesome.

We're in and out of the water several times throughout the action, as the whales sometimes move too far away and we have to reboard to catch up with them. They always seem to move as though they know where we are and are being careful not to get too close to us, but also not really caring that we're intruding. I have the impression that we are really irrelevant to them. A half-hour into it, one of the males bows out of the action, leaving just Bruiser and the other smaller male still jousting. Eventually they become less active and move farther away, so we leave them to their own devices. We never do find out who won the lady. Or perhaps she finally got tired of the antics of the big oafs and cruised off to find someone more couth and suave in his courting.

Early in this encounter, I had to make some decisions: try for underwater photos, surface photos, or none. I opted for none. I didn't want to shoot surface because I really wanted to be in the water to witness the events. And I figured the action was too fast and furious for me to get any in-water shots, and I'd probably miss a lot of the action by trying. So I just grabbed my fins, jumped in, and immersed myself in the action. I swam like hell to keep up with them. I've never regretted that decision. The experience of being in the ocean, in the midst of over 100 collective tons of whale testosterone raging and battling within 50 feet under and around me is the most extraordinary thing I've ever witnessed. The images of this Battle of the Titans are seared into my brain.

Friday, Our Departure Day

I'm sitting alone topside at 5:30 a.m. The moon has set. The Big Dipper has wheeled itself high in the night, handle pointed up, spilling millions of stars across a cloudless sky. The boat swings slowly on its mooring in the winds, pointing north, then swinging to point east. The western horizon still holds the faint afterglow of the moon. Low in the east, Venus is so bright that it shines a path on the water.

We will loose our moorings at first light and head south for the Dominican Republic. It's far too dangerous to travel at night through the Bank. There are huge coral bommies everywhere, many of which break the surface at low tide. If we were foolish enough to try it, we would suffer the same fate as the old rusting wreck that has been our only landmark these past five days.

The wind blows strong and steady now out of the north. All along the eastern horizon, a low bank of clouds sits like a mountain range, above which a line of small, slender cumulus clouds drifts north to south, a caravan of wispy white whales, slow and silent. I stand on the bow for a long time to escape the lights and the noise of the generators. I listen to the restless slap, slop, whoosh of the whitecaps around us, punctuated now and then by the soft comforting swoosh of a hump-back's breath. The dawn sky slowly pales behind the whale caravan now, with just a hint of blush washed above the cloud-mountains, outlining the masts of the wreck. In the pale dawn light, I can see occasional spouts off in the distance. The horizon whales are active, as always.

For 5 days now, our entire universe has been 8 miles wide, 60 feet deep and infinitely high, a restless, constantly changing world of blue and white and black, populated with fabulous white-winged black behemoths of unimaginable grace and power. For the whales, this has been merely a part of their annual spring break festivities. They sing their songs, fight epic battles, protect and nurse their young, and play in their great oceanic bathtub. Amid this eons-old oceanic Mardi Gras, we are insignificant intruders.

But what an extraordinary privilege it has been to participate in such a grand party! All that I have seen and experienced these past five days flickers and replays in my mind, and I know I'll cherish these memories and images as long as I live.

CHAPTER 9

TIME TO GO DIGITAL

Paul

These days, ocean lovers, including many divers and snorkelers, are conservation-oriented and follow the axiom: take only photos, leave only bubbles. Translation: do not disturb the underwater environment or remove anything from the ocean. Even taking an empty shell might eliminate the future home for a growing hermit crab seeking larger quarters; just leave your clean bubbles, no trash, as the only evidence of your temporary visit.

With that in mind, I brought my underwater film camera when Carol and I decided to travel to a special destination for our 30th anniversary. Digital photography was just coming into its own. We'd visited many Caribbean Islands, and although we considered a European vacation, we were still beach bums at heart. Consequently, romantic Hawaii was our choice. Our three-island itinerary was Maui, then Kauai, and since I grew up watching *Victory at Sea*, Oahu, to visit Pearl Harbor and see the USS Arizona Memorial.

This wasn't primarily a dive vacation, so my regulator and BC would not make the trip. But we did bring the basics: masks, snorkels, fins, and wetsuits. Our hotel in Maui was the Kanapali Hotel, billed as *The Most Hawaiian Hotel in Maui*. Situated on beautiful Kanapali

Beach, it lived up to its reputation.

Next to the Kanapali Hotel is the Sheraton, built next to a natural peninsula formation called Black Rock, which juts several hundred yards out from the beach. This is also the spot where shore dives start from the beach and continue out along the formation, around the other side of the peninsula and back. It is a shallow dive, where you spend most of the time between 20 and 40 feet.

Carol and I snorkeled the beach along Black Rock and found the snorkeling fabulous. Many fish were new to us, resembling their Caribbean cousins in body type but very different in their color patterns. We saw the Pacific version of triggerfish, surgeonfish, tangs, butterflyfish, and parrotfish darting in and around coral formations. The urchins were also different. In addition to the familiar spiny varieties we see in the Caribbean, many had red spines as thick as pencils, hence their name, pencil urchins. Close to Black Rock itself, the water was somewhat murky with seaweed and surged against the rocks, making it difficult to snorkel safely. But a large mass caught Carol's eye. She pointed, and I saw it was a large green sea turtle, happily munching on seaweed growing on the rocks. It was unperturbed by our presence, and we enjoyed a long encounter watching it eat a leisurely lunch.

Since there was so much interesting sea life within easy reach, I decided to try a shore dive. I signed up at the local dive shack and arranged to rent a regulator and BC. The morning of the dive, the dive-master Kenny and I waded into the surf along with the beachgoers. The dive plan was to swim out from the beach parallel to Black Rock, go past the tip, explore the other side, then reverse course and return to our starting point. Leaving the beach, we moved along the bottom, pulling ourselves along by digging our fingers into the sand to make headway against a strong current. Farther out, the current subsided and we easily swam along the bottom. Immediately, we encountered numerous large turtles sleeping, eating, and going about their day. We also saw a wide variety of urchins, spotted moray eels, and cottonmouth morays, a species I had never encountered before. I had my trusty Sea & Sea MX-10 camera loaded with a 24-shot roll of Kodak film. I happily snapped away, always mindful to try and save a shot or two for the end of the dive because I never knew what I might encounter. Remember, this was back in 2004. Digital cameras were just coming into their own and beginning to displace film, but many people, like me, stubbornly clung to the older medium. Working with film felt more artistic, and the quality was just as good as, if not better than, digital at the time. The obvious advantage that digital photographers enjoyed was shooting to their hearts' content without worrying about running out of shots.

Toward the end of my dive, I monitored the film counter as I took photos #20, #21, #22. I knew I had two shots remaining. *Well, here's an interesting coral formation* —#23. *One left.* Kenny was gesturing toward a cottonmouth moray that posed with his white mouth wide open. I had taken the eel's picture earlier, but we were almost at the end of our dive. *What the heck, we're ready to head back.* Click, #24.

Minutes later, finning around the tip of Black Rock, I started to turn toward the beach, when Kenny swam out toward deeper water. He had spied another large turtle resting on the bottom. I followed. When he approached the turtle, it remained calm and still. Most turtles move away as a diver approaches. Not this one. *He sure looks a lot like ET*, I thought, getting closer. Finally, I reached Kenny and ET. They were together, face-to-face, or face mask to beak. I moved closer, approaching from the side. Kenny inched closer to the turtle; ET inched closer to Kenny. Kenny moved a little closer, ET extended his neck. They were now inches apart, staring at each other. The water was crystal clear with no current to stir the sand.

It was the perfect National Geographic picture. I knew this photo would definitely grace the cover of *Scuba* magazine, a surefire underwater photo contest winner. I raised the camera and carefully composed the shot with both Kenny and ET framed in a great profile. ET's nose was an inch from Kenny's face mask. My mind's eye had already visualized the photo's caption: *Here's Lookin' at You, Kid.* I pressed the shutter. Nothing happened.

Kenny waited; finally he motioned, waving his hand. *Come on Paul, take the shot!* He turned and looked at me.

I pointed to the camera and shrugged. *Out of film!* I looked at ET who had become impatient, like a temperamental actor waiting for his scene cue. He calmly turned and swam away. I watched the shot of a lifetime disappear into the blue. Swimming toward the beach, I was depressed, thinking about the photo op I missed. I decided, *It was time to go digital.*

CHAPTER 10

Attack of the Killer Harp Snail

Judy

Through all the years we've been diving, one of the things Jon and I have enjoyed greatly has been the ability to photograph gorgeous reefs and strange creatures. And like my coauthor, we wrestled with the pros and cons of transitioning from film to digital. Jon and I did finally retire our two Nikonos 35mm film cameras about eight years ago, giving in to the convenience of digital technology. I admit it's nice not having to worry about running out of film, although we still miss the clarity, intensity, and depth/range of color that slide film offered. (And of course, even though we can't run out of film, we've discovered that we still miss shots by running out of battery power.)

I was using my Nikonos in 2000 when we first experienced the marvels of muck diving. I had never even heard of muck diving until the fall of 1999 when we began making plans for our vacation the following spring. We had chosen Papua New Guinea (PNG) as our destination because of its reputation for having exceptionally beautiful, unspoiled reefs with some of the greatest biomass and biodiversity of any ocean area in the world. The woman who first told me about muck diving was an experienced diver who had been to PNG a number of times and was very enthusiastic about this particular variant of sport diving. She effectively communicated the strength of her enthu-siasm but didn't provide me with any meaningful description of what, exactly, muck is. I had visions of swimming through something akin to pea soup, groping along an unseen bottom by feel. Why in the world would anyone be so enthusiastic about that?

What we discovered in PNG was that the term "muck" is used to describe a shallow, sloping bottom composed of either fine sand or coarse silt, devoid of corals but usually sparsely decorated with short sea grasses, small rocky outcrops, and the occasional pile of timber and other human-generated debris. Typically, the water itself is crystal clear, providing you are careful to keep your fins up above the bottom as you swim along. Within this environment lives a remarkable variety of sea life: various colors of sea horses, sea pens, pipefish, anemones and their resident anemone fish; sentinel gobies with blind shrimp as their roommates; lionfish, hermit crabs, and a multitude of fish including a rare little creature called the Diamond Leatherjacket; and schools of razorfish, which seem to disappear into thin air (or rather thin water) when they turn sideways.

With its myriad of small, strange creatures and the lack of large beautiful reef-scapes, muck diving is particularly suited to close-up camera work, and I was well prepared. I had an assortment of close-up extension tubes that attached to the front of the camera. Each tube was paired with a wire framer that jutted out from the front to show exactly where the camera would focus and how large an area would be within the frame of the photo. For those of our readers who have never seen anything other than digital cameras with their auto-zoom and auto-focus features, I'm sure this old Nikonos rig sounds truly bizarre. And it was. But it worked. Mostly.

It worked well for corals, nudibranchs, and other small creatures that couldn't move very fast. All one had to do was position the camera so the metal framer surrounded the subject, and then push the but-ton to take the photo (one professional photographer we met called this technique "smash and flash"). However, the rig was useless for small fish because they would get spooked by the metal framer and disappear into the far-away blue well before the photographer put finger to button.

On these PNG muck dives, I automatically zeroed in on slow-moving targets that couldn't dash away in fear. But then on one dive, I was startled to learn that even slow-moving targets are not necessarily inert or indifferent to being photographed.

On this particular muck dive, a night dive, I found a large harp snail stalking the muck for a meal. Although its shell was only about three inches in diameter, the snail's mantle was a good six or seven inches across, spreading out on the sandy bottom as the creature glided along. I approached slowly and cautiously, gently positioned the five-inch wide metal framer of my close-up camera slightly in front of the animal and snapped the first photo. Not surprisingly, the flash startled the snail and it reacted quickly, gathering in its mantle. I moved in closer and positioned the framer so it enclosed both mantle and shell. As I snapped the second shot, the animal reared up and lunged toward the framer as though to attack! Not wishing to have a large, angry snail plastered to my camera or cruising up my arm, I decided that two shots were quite sufficient.

The Harp Snail Lunges Directly Toward Me   Milne Bay, Papua New Guinea
Judith Hemenway Photo ©

When I later checked an onboard reference book, I discovered that the harp snail is carnivorous, using its mantle to suffocate crabs for its meals. (Luckily, my framer is immune to such tactics.) If some other creature attacks it, the snail can discard the large back portion of its mantle like a lizard discarding its tail. Apparently, this particular snail didn't consider me much of a threat, since it kept both its wits and its mantle and simply schlepped off into the darkness in a huff while I looked to other, hopefully less hostile, subjects.

CHAPTER 11

WHALES 'NEATH THE SOUTHERN CROSS: A "BOOMER" LOOKS AT 60

Paul

Depending on how we engage life, our journey can be well planned out, totally random, or somewhere in between. For most people, I suspect it leans toward the latter. For me I would say, moderately serendipitous.

Case in point. This adventure resulted from a gift I sent to diver and author Bonnie Cardone, a member of The Women Divers Hall of Fame. During December 2004, I had mailed Bonnie several copies of *Dangerous Waters*, as a Christmas present. She had been kind enough to read and review the original manuscript, provide invaluable feedback, and even more invaluable encouragement. Sending Bonnie that gift ultimately led me to the greatest adventure of my life so far—a journey to the South Pacific to swim with the humpback whales that traverse the Southern Ocean between Antarctica and Tonga.

The morning of February 11, 2005, I received the following e-mail from a total stranger:

Hi Paul,

My friend Bonnie Cardone gave me a copy of *Dangerous Waters* as a Christmas present, and I really enjoyed reading it. Thanks for creating such a wonderfully strong and engaging female character! When will your next book be out? Do you have a mailing list that you can add me to, so I'll know when it's available?

Best wishes to you!
Judy Hemenway
www.divingturtle.com

Judy's e-mail began a continuing friendship that has endured through reading and reviewing my next three novels, *Whales' Angels, Fireworks,* and *Near Miss,* and now our joint venture, *Bubbles Up.*

During the latter half of 2006, Judy e-mailed information to me about a trip she and her husband, Jon, were planning for 2007: Ten days cruising the South Pacific Tonga Islands on the 120-foot motor/sail live-aboard dive schooner *Nai'a* (in Hawaiian *nai'a* means "dolphin") to swim with humpback whales.

Jimmy Buffett's book, *A Pirate Looks at Fifty,* was still fresh in my mind and provided inspiration for this adventure. Jimmy's family had sent him on an Amazonian jungle river trip for his 50th birthday, so I jumped at the chance to celebrate my 60th by heading to the South Pacific to play with the whales.

My flight itinerary was American Airlines from New York's JFK to Los Angeles' LAX airport. During a three-hour layover in Los Angeles, I would join Judy and Jon, neither of whom I had ever met in person. Then, we all would fly Air Pacific from Los Angeles to Fiji and finally to Nuku'alofa on Tongatapu, Tonga's largest island. There we would meet up with the *Nai'a,* our live-aboard dive boat.

An aircraft equipment problem in New York ate up my entire three-hour planned layover. Arriving late in Los Angeles, I barely had time to catch the Air Pacific flight. I sprinted the last 200 yards to the waiting 747 just as the crew started closing the door. After takeoff, I ventured upstairs to the giant plane's second deck and met Judy and Jon for the first time. They were both sure I had missed the flight.

This adventure became even more challenging thanks to American Airlines. I arrived in Tonga, south of Fiji, with nothing but the clothes on my back, the cameras in my carry-on luggage, and Judy and Jon's psychological and emotional support. The airline had sent my two checked bags carrying dive equipment, clothing, toiletries, etc. on their own worldwide trip. Many times after my South Pacific adventure, I have looked at my eventually-returned, mute bags, wishing they could speak and tell me about their travels.

Luckily for me, we were scheduled to stay in Tonga's capital, Nuku'alofa, for two days waiting for the *Nai'a* to arrive. John, the driver who picked us up at the airport, volunteered to take me on a shopping spree of Tongatapu Island to replace the clothing and other necessities that were traveling the globe, courtesy of American Airlines. He also treated Judy, Jon, and me to a private tour of the island.

One morning we awoke to see the *Nai'a* anchored just off shore. Seeing her in person for the first time, floating in the harbor that was empty the day before, heightened my sense of anticipation. I was excited to finally see the boat that would soon take us to meet the whales. The *Nai'a's* crew spent the day provisioning her for our 10-day trip, and later that afternoon our 16-person group departed north toward the whale grounds.

Tonga's 170 islands constitute a whale sanctuary. Humpbacks begin arriving from their Antarctic feeding grounds around June to mate, give birth, and relax in the tropics. Underwater visibility routinely exceeds 100 feet, giving our encounters a very different feel from my previous experience swimming with whales in the Dominican Republic's relatively shallow and murkier Silver Bank.

We encounter humpback whales every day, both above and below the surface of Tonga's azure, several-hundred-feet-deep, crystal-clear waters. During surface encounters, we are treated to spectacular humpback behaviors: whales breaching, hurling their 40-ton bodies clear of the water, then crashing back in a foamy explosion; mother whales teaching their calves tail slapping (smashing massive tail flukes against the surface); and pec-fin slapping (rolling onto their sides and whacking their 10- to-15-foot-long pectoral fins down onto the water).

Underwater encounters with these aquatic giants are the stuff of imagination. You swim so closely to them that you can see them rotate their eye in your direction, and you know they are watching you. You are in awe of their size and power, as you watch their long pec fins and broad flukes moving with purpose.

Scuba diving here, as in other whale sanctuaries, is not permitted with whales, so we freedived with fins, mask, and snorkel. Totally submerged, whales take on a different character. When observed on the surface, they appear as lumbering submarines. Underwater, they become totally weightless, transforming themselves into sinuous, graceful "dancers."

Frequently, these massive 40- to 50-foot giants slow down and swim with us, curiously inspecting the strange, tiny, split-fin creatures with what appeared amusement. Sometimes the whales stay deep and John, one of our divers, freedives down to them, enticing them to rise from the depths and engage us.

John Coaxes a Humpback to the Surface   Tonga, South Pacific
Paul Mila Photo ©

While John plays with one whale, I watch two others on my left, circling each other like sinuous dancers. Suddenly, a surge of water rocks me. I glance to my right, just as another massive humpback surfaces next to me. We meet, eye-to-eye, human and whale sharing the same space for a brief magical moment in time.

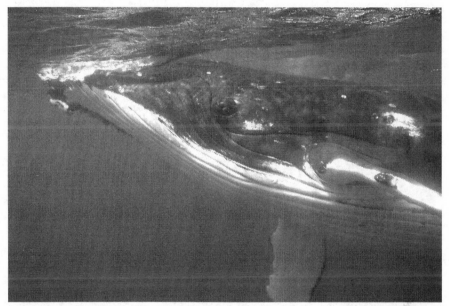

Swimming with a Giant   Tonga, South Pacific
Paul Mila Photo ©

Floating next to a living, breathing creature 40 feet long and weighing 40 tons provides a lesson in humility. I am too awed to feel fear. From previous encounters, I've learned that if the whales know you are close, they take great care not to hit you with their pec fins and tail flukes. The whale pauses and looks at me while filling his huge, car-size lungs. When you are so close to a whale that you can hear him breathe and feel its misty exhalation fall like oily raindrops, you can feel his life force. You realize you are not next to some super-sized inanimate movie prop.

The humpback swims along the surface, letting me tag along. I pump my fins as fast as I can, trying to keep pace. There we are, human and whale swimming next to each other. I look at the whale, and he looks back at me. Occasionally, he blinks. (Yes, whales can blink their eyes; they have eyelids and eyebrows.) I thought, *This is incredible. I'm actually swimming next to a giant Pacific humpback!*

After several minutes, I think the whale grows bored. He glances at me once more with a softball-sized eye and curiosity satisfied, arches his back and heads for the deep. I watch him disappear, 10-foot-wide flukes pumping gracefully, rhythmically, powering this amazing being from an aquatic world down into the deep blue where I cannot follow. I wonder what the whale thought during our brief encounter. I suspect that he was not as impressed with me as I was with him.

The next morning, we spot several humpbacks swimming near the *Naia*. They are so close that instead of venturing out in our Zodiacs, we jump into the water. Looking into the 300-foot-deep water, I see a whale rise up like a ghostly apparition, his white belly reflecting the sunlight. I take a deep breath and dive down to take a photo of the whale as it rolled, passing only 20 feet below, belly up. *Naia* owner, Rob Barrel, shoots video and catches me taking the shot.

I Freedive with a Whale   Tonga, South Pacific
Photo Courtesy of Rob Barrel from Video ©

It is an unusual photo, a close-up showing the whale's ventral grooves. When a baleen whale is feeding, these grooves open like the pleats of a skirt, or an accordion, allowing the whale to engulf tons of water and the small crustaceans, usually krill, that make up his diet. The whale then strains out the water using the baleen plates, which hang from his upper jaw, like a sieve, and swallows the food in one gulp.

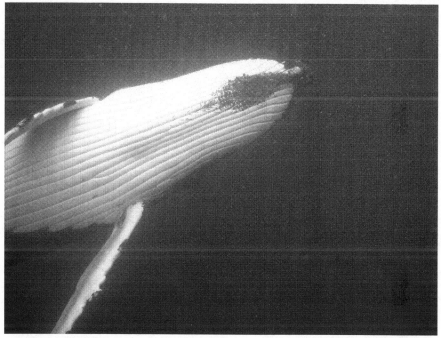

A Humpback's Ventral Grooves   Tonga, South Pacific
Paul Mila Photo ©

This angle also provides a good view of the "barnacle beard" that this group of humpbacks acquires during their travels between the South Pacific and Antarctic oceans. Barnacles attach themselves to many whale species, usually at the larval stage of their existence. Why the tiny creatures pick this particular location on these whales is not known but may involve the consistent water flow over this part of the whale's body.

A couple of days later, I decide to practice freediving to improve my underwater breath-holding skills. Catching a breath at the surface, I spot a pair of humpbacks cruising less than 50 yards away. I duck my head below the water to get an underwater view, breathing through my snorkel. One of the pair veers toward me, so I take several deep breaths and then dive, hoping for a good underwater photo angle.

The unpredictable nature of wildlife photography is that you never know what's going to happen. Sometimes you're in the wrong place at the wrong time; or you might be in the right place at the right time, but your subject decides not to cooperate.

But this time the magic happens. I am in the right place at the right time, and my whale plays his part to perfection. When I raise my camera and look through the viewfinder, I see the giant humpback approaching directly toward me. The whale, as big as a bus but graceful as a greyhound, spreads its long, white pectoral fins like an eagle in flight and turns toward the surface, giving me a firsthand glimpse why humpbacks have the official Latin name *Megaptera novaeangliae.* (Translation: Giant Winged of New England.) My lungs are burning for air when I take the photo, and we surface together. I hear a strong whooshing breath

Megaptera novaeangliae Sporting a Barnacle Beard   Tonga, South Pacific
Paul Mila Photo ©

behind me, but when I turn, all I see is misty spray and a fluke slipping beneath the waves as the whale dives to rejoin his partner.

This was the way we spent our days, sailing among the Tongan Islands, one of which was the real location for the actual "mutiny on the bounty." But Rob Barrel had nothing to fear here. We were all a happy bunch, and mutiny was the last thing on our minds.

When the whales were not present, we scuba-dived on seamounts, the tops of underwater mountains rising to within 60 to 80 feet below the surface. Around us, the sea was filled with the mournful sounds of whale songs as they communicated with each other. But since sound travels far underwater, radiating in all directions, the whales remained out of sight. Sometimes their calls sounded so loud we expected to bump into a whale around the next coral head, but we never saw our singers.

One of the older divers in our group, a man in his 70s who had explored the seamounts with us, was content to remain in the Zodiac when we visited the whales. Summing up his adventure, he expressed his feelings more eloquently than I could.

He said, "Now I can die happy. I've been close to a whale."

In the evenings, Judy, her husband Jon, and I joined the crew in their front cabin. We listened to them sing Pacific Islander songs and we all drank kava, a social and ceremonial drink made from the root of the kava plant.

Our 10-day adventure ended all too soon. I spent our last night on deck, stretched out on a lounge, watching streaking meteors pierce the Southern Cross constellation. The silence was broken by the occasional blow of a humpback near the boat, resting on the surface. Reflecting on our adventure, I hoped I would come back some day to visit the whales.

But if not, I am satisfied that I experienced another lifetime dream: swimming with Pacific humpback whales!!

CHAPTER 12

A SENSE OF FAMILY

Judy

Before Jon and I left on our whale-watching trip to Tonga with Paul, my 84-year-old father and my brother Johnny and I were talking. Dad said, "If something happens to me while you're gone, don't cut your vacation short to come back. I won't be here anyhow!"

Johnny agreed. "I'll take care of everything till you get home, so don't worry about it."

We joked about maybe keeping him on ice—he'd always had a delightfully warped sense of humor—but I fully expected him to still be there when we got home. I knew he was nearing the end, but he was a tough old bird and stubborn to boot. I looked forward to sharing photos and stories of our adventures with him. He always really enjoyed that. But I was also glad that Johnny had agreed to be there the whole time we were gone. I knew I could depend on him, and I couldn't have left otherwise.

So when we got word of Dad's death, we were in the middle of the South Pacific, 5,000 miles from home, and a 15-hour boat ride from the nearest airport with only the boat's emergency satellite phone as a link to the outside world. I was stunned by the news, and I felt lost and adrift in an alien world. Other than our boat's 16 passengers and

14 crew, we had seen no other humans, no other boats, not even any airplanes, in 8 days. Most of the crew were Fijians, half of the passengers were Russian, and the islands we cruised around were part of the Kingdom of Tonga. Jon and Paul—and that satellite phone—were my only anchors. Even more disorienting was the fact that we were on the other side of the International Dateline, so it was already 6:00 p.m. Monday evening for me, even though it was only 10:00 p.m. Sunday evening back home. It had only taken a few hours for my niece Jenny's e-mail to get to me, but it seemed like it had been days. I wanted to be home, in familiar surroundings, with the comfort of my family and friends. It just didn't seem right, and yet . . .

Rob, the boat owner, gave me immediate access to the satellite phone. The trip director, Sonia, a native of Colombia, South America, hugged and kissed me like a sister. Igor, who could barely speak English, looked at me with the kindest eyes and gave me a big Russian bear hug, while his sister Olga translated. The captain let me know that if I needed anything, I should just ask, and Suli, our steward, gave me comfort with soft words about loss and the treasuring of memories. Big, grave John, the chief engineer, said not a word but looked deep into my eyes with such kindness and sympathy that no words were needed. In short, everyone, both passengers and crew, closed around me like a big downy comforter and became my family.

I couldn't sleep that night, so I got up about 3:00 a.m. and sat down with my journal. I felt this compulsion to understand what I had been doing, where I was, while Dad was dying. I went back over my entries for the past few days, working out what time it was back home. While Dad was living out his last day, we spent the entire day out in the middle of the ocean with no land in sight. We swam with a mother humpback and her young calf. We could hear the singing of the whales, which is part of their courtship. At one point, we swam for a half-hour or so with a group of eight or nine large whales. Later, we dived on an underwater pinnacle called Palako's Patch. Then we moved in close to one of the uninhabited islands and went ashore to do some beachcombing.

Dad would have gotten a big laugh out of the four-foot-tall stick that some previous beachcomber had planted in the sand and decorated with all the old derelict flip-flops that had washed up on the beach. At dinner that evening, we sat with Dimitri and his 10-year-old daughter, Sonia. I know Dad would have appreciated hearing Dimitri talk about his daughter with such love and pride and bemusement. When Dad took his last breath, we were in the middle of watching Rob's video of the whales that he had taken that day. Perhaps when Dad slipped away, he was able to stop by and watch it with us. He would have been delighted to be able to see it so clearly, after so many years of being almost blind.

Rob told me that in the 11 years he has been doing these whale trips, he has never seen such close and extensive interaction between whales and humans as we experienced on this trip. He wondered if maybe it was Dad's energy manifesting itself in them. I told Rob that if there was any way that Dad could give such a gift, he would.

Baby Humpbacks Stay Close to Their Mothers   Tonga, South Pacific
Judith Hemenway Photo ©

After we ended our voyage among the whales, we spent several days on the largest island of the kingdom and learned much about the Tongan people and their culture. The more I talked with them and learned from them, the more I realized that Tonga was not such an alien land. Dad would have felt right at home there.

Like Dad, the Tongans are a warm and genuinely friendly people, to whom family means more than anything. Like Dad, they are extraordinarily generous, giving even when they have nothing. Like Dad, their approach to life is simple and straightforward, with much laughter and music.

I learned too about Tongan funerals. If we were Tongan, my brother Johnny would be the *ulumotua*—the oldest person in the family, the one who presides over the funeral service. As the oldest auntie of the family, I would be the *fahu*—the guest of honor, and it would be my oldest niece, Jenny, who would sit next to Dad's remains. It is the *fahu's* responsibility to be the *lohu loa*—the one who keeps the family connected with each other across the years and across whatever miles may separate them.

My "Family" on Board the *Nai'a* Including Coauthor Paul   Tonga, South Pacific
(Back—Second from Left)
Photo Courtesy of Jon Fellows ©

So across 5,000 miles of ocean in an alien land, I found a sense of family, of home. In the midst of the heartache I felt, and the great sense of loss, I also experienced the kindness of strangers and the incredible magic of communing with the great-winged whales as I floated in an ocean that was filled with their singing.

CHAPTER 13

AQUATIC ADVENTURES IN FATHER-DAUGHTER BONDING

Paul

M any families create their most lasting memories vacationing by the ocean. Some blow bubbles together beneath the waves, others snorkel among sea creatures as they glide over a colorful reef, or perhaps they just enjoy spending quality time together at a beach or seaside resort. Carol and I introduced our daughters, Christine and Laura, to the wonders and beauty of the sea as early in their lives as possible. That meant frequent visits to the beach when they were barely toddlers, trips to aquariums, whale watching off Montauk, Long Island, and many Caribbean vacations. These two adventures are among my favorite memories:

Christine

When Christine was ten and Laura eight, we vacationed in Key West, Florida. One day we decided to go on a snorkeling trip. Actually, it was a combination scuba and snorkel trip (I realized later a bad idea for the snorkelers) to a reef 15 miles offshore. At that point in my life, I was not yet a scuba diver. Carol and I had taken snorkel trips before, but never a combo scuba trip. And most of our experience involved snorkeling offshore in calm bays but never far out in the open ocean. This trip was to a reef that popped up somewhere in the Atlantic.

The routine was for the scuba folks to suit up and enter the water first. That meant we snorkelers turned green getting seasick while the anchored boat pitched to and fro until it was our turn to jump in. By that time, Carol and Laura were in no mood to snorkel, so Christine and I went. We felt much better once we were off the boat. Barfing in the water also helped. I heard Laura shouting from the boat, "Daddy, Daddy, look, Mommy's feeding the fish!" We looked back and saw Carol leaning over the rail, head down. A large school of jacks, snappers, chubs, and sergeant majors were enjoying a mini feeding frenzy as "food" rained down upon them.

The captain told us he would sound the horn after 40 minutes, indicating we must return to the boat, after which the scuba divers would reboard and we would depart. Christine and I headed out to explore the reef 25 feet below us. I was amazed at how effortless the snorkeling was. We looked at the colorful coral and sponges passing below us and enjoyed watching a variety of interesting fish whose colors were as diverse as the reef. After 30 minutes, I told Christine we should head back to the boat. We turned back and saw there were now several dive boats moored near ours, almost all identical. We started finning toward the fleet. Christine was totally absorbed in the experience, enjoying the underwater scenery and sea life.

Then I heard the horn blare, which meant we needed to return immediately. I saw that the boats were still hundreds of yards away. I started kicking harder, though now my legs felt like lead. After 10 minutes, the little flotilla did not seem any closer. I looked down and saw that even as we were kicking hard, the bottom was not moving. We were basically going nowhere. Only then did I realize we had been swimming with the current on the way out, hence the effortless swim. Now, we were trying to swim against the current.

A more experienced snorkeler would have done the reverse, swimming against the current at the start and enjoying an easy swim back to the boat at the end. I was tiring and becoming concerned that we wouldn't make it back. Saltwater filled my leaky mask, stinging my eyes, and I couldn't make out which boat was ours. As I kicked harder, my anxiety level rose. The only thing preventing me from having a panic attack was watching Christine. I held her hand, pulling her along as we both kicked. She was totally oblivious, trusting that Dad had everything under control. I realized "losing it" was not an option. She was as happy and unconcerned as a minnow in a tidal pool. Of course, the minnows don't realize that when the tide recedes and the sun begins evaporating their little oasis, they're in big trouble.

We continued kicking together, momentarily distracted and awed as a pair of silvery-blue great barracuda, I estimated at least four-feet long, glided effortlessly below us. Knowing Christine was counting on me to get us safely back made me bear down, kick harder, and forget I was pretty much out of breath. Eventually, the bottom moved a little faster, and somehow I navigated back to the correct boat. We boarded the rocking boat and turned green once again, while waiting for the scuba divers to surface and clamber aboard.

Years Later, Paul and Christine Celebrate After Snorkeling   Cozumel, Mexico
Paul Mila Photo ©

My most vivid memory of that trip was seeing how unconcerned Christine was, trusting that I had the situation well in hand. It was one of those *Father Knows Best* moments that pass too quickly and then disappear forever when children enter their teen years and parents turn into "uncool" beings.

These days, in her mid-30s, Christine still enjoys snorkeling with me. But now, more cautious with age, or just plain smarter, she usually swims the other way when encountering fish bigger than we are, or when I try to convince her to join me following a stingray.

Laura

My younger daughter, Laura, eventually took our water-world experiences one step further. She had listened to my underwater adventure stories and seen my photographs and videos. During her senior year at the College of William & Mary, she took a course in kinesiology. One of the options within the course was a scuba certification, which she elected to take. When I asked her reasoning, she was very forthright.

"Well, I figured sometimes you'll need a dive buddy, so that means free trips for me."

Smart kid. As my mother, Rose, once said, "I didn't raise a fool."

Laura finished her pool and classroom work, and the final certification step required four open water dives. She could have completed them at college in Virginia or in the New York area. But we felt diving in gin-clear, warm Caribbean water would be preferable to bumping into the remains of someone's rusty '58 Edsel, in cold, murky northeastern water. So I contacted my instructor Alison in Cozumel and arranged for her to complete Laura's open water certification in a tropical paradise.

The first open water exercises require the student to demonstrate basic snorkeling techniques and the ability to be comfortable swimming underwater as a freediver without equipment. Then, more difficult exercises follow, such as mask clearing, which requires the student to remove and replace the mask underwater.

Alison watched Laura complete the exercises with ease and then scolded me. "She swims like a fish! Why didn't you do this years ago?"

Gee, I figured I was doing pretty well as scuba-dad. After all, Laura was about 30 years ahead of me in learning how to dive. I hadn't gotten

Laura Performs Mask Clearing for Alison   Cozumel, Mexico
Paul Mila Photo ©

certified until my 50s. "Well, Alison, it's like this. Life just got in the way, you know?"

Anyway, Laura proved to be a natural at scuba and easily passed her certification dives. She was relaxed, sometimes too much so, and mastered the more difficult aspects of diving, like buoyancy control, with ease.

Over the past several years it has been a thrill to have my daughter with me as a dive buddy. Of course we have had our strains. For example, when I point to my air gauge as a signal for Laura to check her gauge and reply with sign language how much air she has left, I sometimes get the "Enough, Dad" eye roll. Then she looks away before I can communicate my air situation back to her. In fact, Laura rarely checks on Dad. I could be frantically making the "slash your throat with your hand" universal dive sign for "out of air" and my dive buddy would never realize I was out of gas. She would glide along with the current, arms folded and ankles crossed, calmly watching the scenery slide by.

Laura has a thrills-and-spills personality. On family vacations, she has pushed me onto the Space Mountain and Water Flume rides in Disney World. I should have known the same thing would happen underwater. When she heard Alison describe diving The Devil's Throat in Cozumel, she said, "Dad, we have to do that dive."

Being more cautious (I call it sensible), I was not so eager.

This dive calls for descending to 85 feet relatively quickly, in order to save air and minutes of no-decompression time. Then you enter an opening in the reef and proceed through a dark, descending, twisting tunnel until you reach the tricky part called The Devil's Throat. Here the tunnel is not much wider than your shoulders, and visibility is only several feet because of sand stirred up by the other divers. The pièce de résistance is that you now must ascend several feet over a mound and then invert yourself head down to pass under the low ceiling and exit the tunnel at 125 feet. All the while, you need to keep moving so you don't spend more time than your dive computer or decompression tables allow at this depth. Otherwise you must perform a decompression stop before surfacing, and you might or might not have sufficient air remaining to do so. This is Laura's idea of fun.

But I had an easy out. Instead of just admitting I was too apprehensive to try the dive, I relied on a tried-and-true formula. "Forget it. Your mother would kill me!"

"But Alison's seventy-year-old mother did it!"

"Okay, ask me again when I'm seventy."

Fast-forward a year later on another trip to Cozumel. Alison was away on vacation, so we were diving with Sand Dollar, the Reef Club Resort's dive operation. The divers that day wanted to dive The Devil's Throat. Laura persisted. .She was now more experienced, so I relented. I spent the 30-minute boat ride to Punta Sur, the reef at the southern end of Cozumel where The Devil's Throat is located, mentally rehearsing how I'll explain this decision to my wife. After, *"But honey . . ."* I'm not having any luck filling in the blank.

There were six of us on the boat: the driver Jose, the divemaster Victor, two other divers, Laura and I. We arrived at the dive site and

Victor went over the dive plan. We performed a backward roll off the boat. The sea was calm, the current unusually mild for Cozumel waters. We performed a last minute safety check on the surface and then descended. Laura headed for the bottom and looked up at me, still near the surface. I have what are called slow-clearing ears. For some medical reason regarding how my Eustachian tubes are built, I must descend slowly, constantly clearing my ears every couple of feet. I soon caught up and we followed Victor into the cave. I looked at my dive computer. It indicated 85 feet and displayed the number "19," which were the minutes we could safely remain at this depth without requiring a decompression stop. We proceeded through the dark tunnel and turned on our flashlights. I said a prayer. *Energizer Bunny, don't fail me now!*

We went deeper, and I checked my computer again. Our minutes of safe time were decreasing faster than actual elapsed time because we were descending: 90 feet, 11 minutes of no-deco time left; 100 feet, 9 minutes. The tunnel widened momentarily into a large cavern, and Victor stopped to shine his flashlight on a yellow tube sponge, shaped like a cross, attached to the cavern wall. I was hoping this wasn't an omen. 105 feet, 8 minutes left. We continued down. Soon the tunnel narrowed again. My shoulders rubbed against the walls, and my tank bumped the ceiling, the metallic scrape very unsettling. I was last in line. If I got stuck no one would know, and there was no way out or up. As my anxiety level rose, I wondered what Laura would tell her mother. *Gee, Mom, I thought Dad was right behind me.*

The other divers were ahead of Laura and me and had kicked up some sand. Even with the flashlight, it was dark, visibility so hazy I could barely see Laura's fins less than two feet ahead of me. I felt my way forward and looked at my dive computer. The readout displayed 120 feet, 4 minutes. We came to the mound. I went up and over, then inverted, head down. 125 feet, only 3 minutes before we would run out of no-decompression time, preventing a direct ascent to the surface without a mandatory stop. Finally, I saw dim light ahead, and then we exited the cave. I looked up and saw a bright light. Fortunately, it was not the light of a near-death experience, just the glorious Caribbean sun shining through the surface.

It's a familiar sight when glancing up from the bottom, but I promised myself I would never take it for granted again. Immediately, but slowly, we ascended to 100 feet, then 90, then 80. Ascending "buys" more decompression time on the computer. We now had 15 minutes, and we continued the dive, slowly ascending as we finned along.

After a 3-minute safety stop at 15 feet, we surfaced. Waiting for the boat to pick us up, Laura exclaimed, "Wasn't that great, Dad?"

"Yeah," I replied, very relieved. I had to admit that Laura had once again pushed me into an adventure I probably would not have experienced on my own. As we climbed aboard our small dive boat, I remarked to Victor, "You really cut the time pretty close. We were still in the cave at a hundred and twenty-five feet and only had less than three minutes before we would have had a decompression situation."

He smiled and shrugged his shoulders. I observed that Victor was not wearing a dive computer.

CHAPTER 14

DIVING INTO HISTORY

Judy

I was 12 years old when the first film version of the Rodgers and Hammerstein musical *South Pacific* hit the screens. Living as I did in a landlocked small town (population roughly 16,000 people) in the midst of central Pennsylvania's vast green farmlands, I had no idea that such a place as the South Pacific existed—until I saw the movie. That was all it took. I was instantly, irrevocably hooked. I read Michener's *Tales of the South Pacific* and *Hawaii*, watched the TV series he created (*Adventures in Paradise*), saw the films *Mutiny on the Bounty* (Fletcher Christian will forever look like Marlon Brandon in my mind's eye) and *Hawaii*.

It took me 32 years to get there the first time, but I have been fortunate enough to have made a half dozen trips to the South Pacific since then. All have been diving trips, and the South Pacific waters are extraordinarily beautiful, teeming with all manner of exotic flora and fauna. I can't imagine ever growing tired of diving those waters, and I will always cherish the photos and memories I've gleaned from them.

As part of every trip, we planned for shore leave—time to explore the islands and the local cultures. For leisure-time reading, we selected books by or about the people and the history of the islands. Of course, Michener's *Tales of the South Pacific* was my starting point, but I had no real grasp of the significance of the military activities and battles he described. Nor did I have the least inkling that I would one day actually visit some of those locations and dive in those waters.

One of the best known of those battles is the Guadalcanal campaign, which began in August 1942. On August 7, the first day of that campaign, in the battle of Tulagi and Ghavutu-Tanambogo (see http:// tinyurl.com/Sol-Campaign-I), five or six Japanese Kawanishi H6K5 "Mavis" seaplanes were shot down. One of them sits on the ocean bottom in about 80 feet of water off of Ghavutu in the Florida (Nggela) Island group (which lies directly north of Guadalcanal).

We had the opportunity to dive the Ghavutu site during our trip to the Solomon Islands in 2010 aboard the *M. V. Bilikiki*. This particular plane was remarkably intact, with only its right wing broken off, resting downslope from the remainder of the plane. There is a marker buoy attached to the nose of the plane, so we were able to drop down right on top of it. We inspected the cockpit area first, and then moved along the fuselage to the left wing. The plane was huge: 84 feet long with a wingspan of 130 feet (when it was intact).

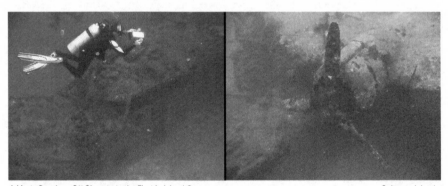

A Mavis Seaplane Off Ghavutu in the Florida Island Group   Solomon Islands
Judith Hemenway Photos ©

At 80 feet down, the entire plane was a study in olive greens and turquoise blues, its cockpit windows a line of gaping, empty rectangles. Unlike shipwrecks, which rapidly develop a vibrant growth of corals, algae, and other marine life, airplanes seem to discourage such colonization, even after almost 60 years. The skin of this Mavis was crusted over with a thin layer of patchy scab-like growths, making it look pale, sickly, and diseased. There was no current, no movement other than our own swimming, no sound other than our own breathing. We did not explore the rear section of the fuselage but cruised slowly out along the left wing to the first of the two massive engines that swelled intact out of the forward edge of the wing, the three blades of its propeller still intact and frozen in place.

As we finned slowly along the length of the wing, I wondered what had happened that terrible fateful day so long ago. Did any of the crew survive? Who had shot it down, and did they survive? According to the Navy website, "The cost of taking Ghavutu and Tanambogo was seventy Marine lives. As on Tulagi, there were few Japanese survivors."

Wars are simply abstract concepts when you read about them in books or on websites. But seeing the empty, silent wrecks makes it palpably, intensely real.

Our next dive was nearby, just off Ghavutu, where the wharf and jetty of the Japanese-held Ghavutu Seaplane Base had once jutted out over the water. A half dozen or so pilings stood sentry, encrusted with corals and rising stolidly 15 to 18 feet from the bottom, their top ends truncated 10 feet below the surface. All around them, the bottom was littered with piles of debris, largely unrecognizable.

As I finned among the debris, I became caught up with the wealth of sea life in the area: fang blennies striped in yellow, black, and white; some lovely transparent tunicates; a large crocodile fish lazing about on a flat piece of wreckage; a sea urchin with striped spines; a heavily encrusted intact teapot; some mating nudibranchs; and a neat little "winged" pipefish.

After the dive, I thought back to that teapot, its image still etched in my mind. Somehow it had survived the bombs and bullets of two days of intense fighting and found its way to the bottom. Over the past 70 years, the corals have slowly accreted, layering the pot in lavender, pink, yellow, green, red, brown, and white, and gently cradling its base in graceful gray ruffles.

An Intact Teapot at Ghavutu Seaplane Base   Solomon Islands
Judith Hemenway Photo ©

The Guadalcanal campaign raged on for six months after the Mavis was shot down and Ghavutu destroyed. The Japanese were based on Bougainville Island to the northwest, and their ships made frequent runs down The Slot to attack Guadalcanal. It was these movements that the coastwatchers reported on, as Michener depicted in "The Cave," with its coastwatcher who was called "The Remittance Man."

The entire stretch of The Slot northwest of Guadalcanal is littered with shipwrecks, including 33 Allied ships (mostly United States) and 14 Japanese ships. Prior to the war, this passage had been called Sealark Channel, but since then, it has come to be known as Ironbottom Sound. Two of the Japanese transport ships are grounded along the coast a short distance northwest of Honiara and are shallow enough to be easily accessible to divers.

We made two dives on the *Hirokawa Maru* and one on the *Kinugawa Maru*. The *Hirokawa Maru* was still largely intact. We descended on the west side, which is roughly the bottom of the ship.

It rests on its side in about 80 feet of water.

We followed the nearly featureless hull down, and then finned around the stern to the east side, which has more features, since it is the deck side. There were huge gaping holes indicating where I imagine portions of the superstructure had once been, railings that jutted upward at awkward angles, large metal spires reaching up toward the surface, a ladder that spanned the top of two large parallel plates, all lavishly encrusted with corals.

In one area, I was able to look through a series of parallel rectangular openings, through some similar openings on the other side to the clear turquoise waters beyond. It was like peering through the ribs of a massive skeleton. One of the spires that reached toward the surface had two parallel horizontal pieces that jutted outward, like a supplicant praying to the sun above.

Two Views of the *Hirokawa Maru* in Iron Bottom Sound   Solomon Islands
Judith Hemenway Photos ©

The *Kinugawa Maru* lies just south of the *Hirokawa Maru* and is easy to spot because there are still a few parts of the superstructure that break the surface, including a tall, narrow, square piece that is very visible. However, much of the wreck has collapsed and disintegrated over the past 70 years, so it is more difficult to discern individual features. A ladder is clearly visible though, lying haphazardly on top of the wreck, its four rungs angled upward toward the shore.

Both ships were heavily encrusted with corals, sponges, anemones, and other fixed sea life, and teeming with mollusks, octopods, nudibranchs, starfish, sea urchins, and fishes of all sorts. Floating along through this astounding scene in the warm tranquil blue waters under a tropical sun, it seems inconceivable that this place could ever have been the scene of such terrible violence, destruction, and death as is described in our history books. The United States had over 100,000 killed or missing and 250,000 wounded in the Pacific Theater. The Japanese had 1.7 million killed or missing and 94,000 wounded. Diving sites such as these provides us with not only exceptional adventures in a beautiful ocean but also exceptional perspectives on human history.

A similar opportunity is provided by another remarkable book that centers on a different culture, the Polynesian culture of Tonga: *An Account of the Natives of the Tonga Islands* by William Mariner. I read this book on our trip to Tonga on the *Nai'a*.

William Mariner was a 15-year-old boy serving as ship's clerk on the British privateer *Port au Prince* when that ship visited the Ha'apai island group of Tonga over 200 years ago. For four years, Mariner lived with the Tongans and in the process learned a great deal about their language, culture, and history. He was an intelligent, perceptive, and articulate young man and after his return to Britain, he set down in writing all that he had experienced and learned.

One of the interesting tidbits we learn from Mariner concerns Captain James Cook's first visit to Lifuka in 1773, a mere 33 years before Mariner's arrival. Cook had been so impressed with the hospitality of the Tongans that he named their domain the Friendly Isles. Mariner learned, however, that their hospitality was illusory. The Tongans had actually planned to kill Cook and his crew during the festivities but failed because they could not agree among themselves on a single plan.

In 2007 (201 years after Mariner's arrival) on our second day aboard the *Nai'a* (see Paul's account of this trip in Chapter 11), we arrived in the Ha'apai island group and made our first anchorage at O'ua Island. We were surrounded by islands, about a half-dozen to the north, a couple scattered to the south. To the NW in the distance, a large flat-topped volcano (Tofua) was visible and a smaller peaked one (Kao). Tofua had blown its top long ago.

We spent several days wandering around among these islands with Tofua and Kao always visible on the horizon.

Tofua on the Left and Kao on the Right Are Visible in the Distance Behind Nearby Fotuha'a Island   Tonga, South Pacific
Photo Courtesy of Jon Fellows ©

One day, as the *Nai'a* rocked gently at anchor off Lifuka, I leaned against the railing and stared out at Tofua. It struck me that we were once again in the middle of history here. Lifuka had been the scene of William Mariner's adventures and Captain Cook's explorations before him, and that mesmerizing, ever-present silhouette of Tofua off on the horizon played an important role in Captain Bligh's misadventures. Tofua was the first landing Bligh made with his loyal followers after they were set adrift by Fletcher Christian and his gang of mutineers on the *Bounty*. In their small open boat, without charts or compass and with little in the way of food and water, they made their way to Tofua in the hopes of finding a supply of fresh water. However, the natives on the island stoned one of the crew, so Bligh and the rest of his crew were forced to continue on with only what they already had.

I'm not sure why, but knowing that I was traveling through the same seas, seeing and visiting the same islands that Bligh, Cook, and

Mariner visited was really a thrill for me. Perhaps because the South Seas have been part of my psyche since I was a teenager, those stories always had the stature of mythology. But being there, seeing the islands and meeting the people, I realized that they were real, and I connected with them in a way that I never had before.

I hadn't planned it. I went diving for adventure, and I found that I had dived into history. I highly recommend it!

CHAPTER 15

DENIZENS OF THE DIVE SHOP

Paul

For many divers, the dive shop is where their adventure began. Some, like me, may have first experienced the wonders beneath the sea during a tropical vacation. Falling under the bewitching spell of swaying palm trees and seduced by the caress of the warm, gin-clear Caribbean, or perhaps just the lingering effect of too many margaritas the previous night, I boldly decided to take what is known as the "resort course" with dive instructor Alison. After a glimpse of the corals, sponges, and undersea inhabitants, I visited Scuba Network, my local dive shop, when I returned home and signed up for lessons.

Perhaps your daily routine takes you past a storefront adorned with the image of a scuba diver or underwater scenes of colorful fish swimming through an undersea garden populated with various sea creatures. The words DIVE LESSONS are prominently displayed in the window. If you are not yet a scuba diver but love the ocean and are thinking about taking the plunge, you should stop in. If you do, your life will be irrevocably altered—for the better. However, if you decide to keep going and not explore what lies behind the door, this chapter will explain what you are missing.

Scuba Network of Long Island   Carle Place, NY
Paul Mila Photo ©

What immediately strikes the uninitiated upon first entering the dive shop is the vast amount of unfamiliar equipment assembled on floor displays and arranged on wall racks throughout the store. Some shops have a separate section for snorkeling gear, which is usually much higher quality than what is found in mall-type sporting goods stores. This section is popular for those on their way to a tropical destination or cruise, typically families on winter holiday breaks and vacations. Frequently, snorkel-gear shoppers will wander around, casually eyeballing the scuba equipment and perhaps reading brochures about scuba lessons. Watching them, you can see that the seed has been planted; germination is in process! It's only a matter of time before they sign up for dive lessons.

The scuba section contains not only familiar products, such as fins, masks, and snorkels, but also various types of diving equipment:

Buoyancy Compensator vests (BCs), regulators, gauges for monitoring air supply and depth, dive computers, wetsuits, and of course, air tanks in a variety of colors. There is also a multitude of accessories: dive knives, signaling devices, clips and lanyards, underwater cameras, etc. Scuba diving is truly the ultimate gadget sport. It can seem overwhelming and confusing at first, but a friendly face quickly reassures you that you will soon understand everything. Indeed, after completing your first lesson you will have assembled equipment, learned how to connect the myriad hoses, and experienced the unfamiliar sensation of breathing underwater. Self-confidence soaring, you are well on your way to becoming a certified scuba diver!

After completing your training and becoming certified, you will visit the dive shop more frequently. The dive shop consistently provides the most "up-atmosphere" you could ever experience anywhere. People stop in for advice, to purchase equipment for an exotic vacation, or to discuss an exciting trip from where they recently returned. Very heady stuff.

There is always something to purchase, equipment to maintain, or additional training to advance your skills. It is not uncommon for a diver to sneak another newly acquired gadget into the house past an unsuspecting, still unconverted spouse or significant other.

But the most attractive aspect of the place is the friendly and upbeat ambiance. Scuba diving is a social sport, and the local dive shop is where interesting and adventurous people congregate, exchange experiences, and make new friends. The dive shop may also sponsor a scuba club and hold monthly meetings where divers meet on a regular basis and form a spirit of camaraderie listening to guest speakers discuss a wide variety of dive-related topics.

For example, Scuba Network on Long Island runs both local dives and exotic scuba adventures to far-flung points of our blue globe. *We Dive the World* is the motto of our dive club, Long Island Network Divers. Our club members return with their passports stamped from Fiji, Galapagos, Maldives, Bahamas, Bonaire, Cozumel, and Belize, among other exotic Planet Ocean locations.

After a while, you eventually realize that the heart and soul of the dive shop is the staff, the owner, sales crew, instructors, assistant instructors, and also the regular visitors who hang around the shop like resident groupers on a reef. These denizens are a collection of the most interesting and eclectic individuals you will ever meet in a single location.

For example, consider the dive instructor whom the prospective divers meet when they arrive for their first lesson. Often, he or she wears relaxed clothing and might appear like a movie character sent from central casting to play the part of a scuba diver. The instructor might wear a cap embroidered with some exotic dive destination and a T-shirt or sweatshirt adorned with the name of the dive shop, a dive club, or some tropical location, but usually not the same place as on the cap. The "uniform" might also include well-worn faded jeans or shorts and finally, water-stained sneakers or boat shoes, perhaps without socks.

The students have no idea about this individual's background. Many assume this is the instructor's primary job. However, most instructors have real careers in areas totally unrelated to scuba diving. Many teach because they love to teach and promote the sport of scuba diving, rather than just to make a little extra money. Case in point, the instructional staff at Scuba Network is a collection of individuals with widely diverse backgrounds. As you can see from the following personal profiles of current and former instructors and staff, scuba diving attracts individuals from all walks of life:

Dive Shop Owner/Instructor: Martha

Former Career: Executive for a cosmetics company.

> "I love teaching people and seeing the excitement in their faces when they get certified. It is fantastic to see how much fun new divers have when I take them on new adventures."

Dive Shop Manager: Bob Werner

Former Career: Management positions in the scuba diving industry, owner of *Planet Earth*, and served in the USAF during Vietnam.

"I enjoy the daily interaction and camaraderie with divers who come into the dive shop."

Bob's impressive dive résumé includes diving the deep WWII wrecks of Truck Lagoon and the pinnacle of northeastern diving, the Italian luxury liner *Andrea Doria,* which rests on the bottom of the cold, dark North Atlantic, 250 feet down.

Dive Instructor: Larry

Real Job: Owner of a management consulting firm, focusing on the personal growth and professional development of the "people side" of business.

"I enjoy introducing and exposing people to new experiences. I love to support people who challenge themselves."

Author's Note: Prior to publication, Larry Mack, one of Scuba Network's best and most beloved dive instructors, passed away. We will miss you, Larry.

Dive Instructor: Matt

Real Job: Auto mechanic.

"I've been teaching twenty-one years because I enjoy sharing my experiences with other people."

Dive Instructor: Rick

Real Job: Real estate management; real estate finance.

"I enjoy teaching because I get to see people grow from having little or no knowledge of scuba diving to becoming fully certified divers."

Dive Instructor: Luis

Real job: Purchasing manager for a major NYC bank.

"I love teaching because I have a passion for scuba diving. I feel a responsibility to pass my knowledge along and keep the sport alive."

Dive Instructor: Stephen

Real Jobs: Executive Director for the Long Island Philharmonic, 2005-2010; President of Arts Marketing Network. Provides management and marketing consulting for symphony orchestras and performing arts organizations.

"I became an instructor because I love to dive and help others gain the ability to share that experience."

Dive Instructor: Karl

Real Job: Computer Programmer/Manager.

"My real job supports my true love—diving. I wanted to share my enthusiasm for diving with others and promote the sport of scuba diving. I derive tremendous joy teaching students how to survive in an alien environment and introducing them to the spectacular underwater world."

Dive Instructor: William

Real Job: Psychotherapist/hypnotherapist in private practice in the NYC/Long Island area.

"My primary focus is helping individuals tune into their inner guidance for answers and support for their life's challenges. I became an instructor because I love diving and I have always loved teaching."

Underwater Photography Instructor/Sales Crew: Paul

Former career: Vice President, MasterCard International, Electronic Payments.

"I love teaching people how to bring home memories with their cameras. In addition, the dive shop atmosphere provides fertile ground for background information I can use writing my dive adventure novels."

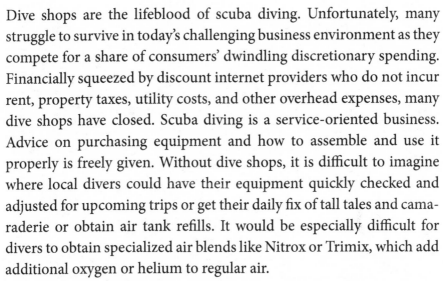

Dive shops are the lifeblood of scuba diving. Unfortunately, many struggle to survive in today's challenging business environment as they compete for a share of consumers' dwindling discretionary spending. Financially squeezed by discount internet providers who do not incur rent, property taxes, utility costs, and other overhead expenses, many dive shops have closed. Scuba diving is a service-oriented business. Advice on purchasing equipment and how to assemble and use it properly is freely given. Without dive shops, it is difficult to imagine where local divers could have their equipment quickly checked and adjusted for upcoming trips or get their daily fix of tall tales and camaraderie or obtain air tank refills. It would be especially difficult for divers to obtain specialized air blends like Nitrox or Trimix, which add additional oxygen or helium to regular air.

Most importantly, dive shops are the primary entry point for new divers. Without attracting and training new divers, the flow of newbies into the sport would dry to a trickle. Resort dive operators, who depend on divers for their livelihood, would feel the immediate impact. But the long-range impact would also be ecological. Many divers, because of their personal interactions with sea life, are enthusiastic advocates for environmental causes to preserve coral reefs and create ocean wildlife sanctuaries. They support legislation to save whales, sharks, and a wide variety of other ocean creatures.

Support Your Local Dive Shop!

CHAPTER 16

HOW TO BE A WET-SET FASHIONISTA

Judy

This chapter is blatantly and unabashedly geared toward female divers.

Diving is exotic, challenging, endlessly variable, exciting, occasionally harrowing, but always—always—fascinating. However, even after more than three decades of pursuing this sport, there was one insight that had escaped me until a fateful two-day dive trip to California's Channel Islands. We were anchored in the middle of the passage between San Miguel and Santa Rosa Islands, an area called the Potato Patch because surface conditions are frequently so rough that when steaming through the area, it feels like the boat is plowing through a very hard and lumpy field. On this particular day, conditions were calm enough to permit anchoring and diving but not without certain challenges, such as trying to maintain your balance on a pitching, heaving deck while weighted down with what felt like tons of gear and at the end of the dive, trying to gain your footing on the swelling, plunging steel mesh swim step, and make it safely back up the ladder to the still pitching and heaving deck.

At the end of our dive, my own performance on the swim step was particularly stellar. When the step dipped low into the swell, I plunged forward on my stomach, beaching myself as gracefully as a slightly pudgy whale, grunted slowly to my knees, unceremoniously dropped my regulator from my mouth, yanked my face mask down around my neck, and wiped my runny, snotty nose on the back of my glove as the crew member on duty pulled my fins off and handed them up the ladder to a second crew member on deck. Slowly and unsteadily I got to my feet, worked my way up the ladder and over to the bench where I plopped down with a sudden thud. My hands were stiff from the cold water, making it a real challenge to get my gloves off and unsnap my tank harness and weight belt. What a relief to shed all that cumbersome stuff! Finally, I pulled off my hood and made a feeble attempt to put my soggy, matted hair in some semblance of order. One of the other women on board who had just gone through a similar ordeal smiled at me and said, "Well, diving certainly isn't a glamour sport, is it!"

That was the moment I had my belated epiphany. Diving is every bit as glamorous and stylish as all the fashion I had seen in the magazines at my nail salon.

I love my nail salon. For me, a fresh pedicure is a little slice of heaven. With the closed-toe shoes I always wear to the office, my engineering colleagues never know that my toenails are all dolled up in *All That Razz-berry* or *Royal Flush Blush*. It's my guilty little secret.

However, I've always had a problem reconciling my image of myself with the images of the women in those magazines. As I would leaf slowly through page after glossy page of *Glamour, In Style* and *Vogue,* I would note the perfectly coifed, air-brushed, artfully made-up, tall, rail-thin models displaying the latest shades and shapes of clothing and accessories and makeup. The more I saw, the more I was aware of my own too-short, aging body, with its 20 extra pounds (okay, 40, if Kate Moss is the measure), and my significantly-less-than-perfectly-stylish wardrobe.

But my epiphany has liberated me. I now realize that Elle McPherson and Paris Hilton and all the rest of the Jet Set Celebutants have nothing on us California Wet-Set Glamazons. No—really. (*Verk vit me on this, Dahlink.*) It's merely a question of thinking outside the boat.

Are you a footwear fetishist, lusting to own the most expensive, stylish, exotic footwear in the world? How about a pair or two of fins?

You have your choice of styles, from basic sling-backs to the daintier and more comfy full-foot fin, the sleek long-blade fin, or that rare and exotic find—the powerful no-nonsense Force Fin. Among the sling-backs, you can choose either closed-toe (the sensible shoe of the Wet Set), or the more alluring and sexy open-toe model. Long-blade fins are divine for creating the illusion that your legs go on forever as you glide silently beneath the surface to gaze into that humpback's eye. But of course, if it's Expensive Exotica that rings your fashion chimes, by all means go for the Force Fins. With their Made-on-Aldebaran styling and almost-stratospheric pricing, you're sure to make a dynamite fashion statement on any reef in the world.

And even the most expensive models, at less than $500, are a bargain, compared to a pair of Manolo Blahniks. So go ahead—splurge—buy several pair! What's that? You fear that flapping around in giant rubber duck feet on a pitching boat deck will make it impossible for you to replicate that blasé, haughty, slouching runway walk? Well, just yesterday, in the middle of New York Fashion Week, one model on three-inch heels with two-inch platform soles did a head-first dive right in the middle of the runway. Girlfriend, walking across a rolling deck in scuba fins is a cakewalk by comparison!

Let's move on now to the central pieces of our Wet-Set ensembles. Of course, the must-have for every woman's wardrobe is the basic "little black dress." For divers, that translates into the basic "puffy black wetsuit," understated but elegant à la Ralph Lauren and suitable for any diving occasion. They come in a variety of thicknesses, from a lightweight wispy 1 millimeter for tropical diving to the cozy 7 mm heft of the California kelp forest wetsuit. With their sleek, body-conscious form, and their suggestively-placed zippers, they are reminiscent of classic Courreges or Donna Karan's revolutionary bodysuit and give every woman that racy, stylish, slightly dangerous aura of *The Avengers'* own Mrs. Emma Peel or Angelina Jolie's *Lara Croft: Tomb Raider*. The fabulous selection of styles and colors ensures that the savvy and sophisticated shopper can turn herself into a veritable goddess of oceanic glamour.

Of course, for those style queens who like pouffy skirts and sleeves, the diving industry has designed the dry suit, an invention that will keep you in the hautest of haute couture even in the depths of the Antarctic. The DUI (no, that's not diving under the influence—it's Diving Unlimited International) is roomy, boxy, with lumps galore, and with its capacity to hold air pumped directly from your scuba tank, can look as pouffy as you want. And at $2,000 or so per suit, it's right up there in the financial stratosphere with the choicest of the chic designer numbers.

Have you been a slave to endless diets in an effort to look like all those emaciated models slinking down the walkways? Well, we divers (and those amazing English Channel swimmers, too) take our inspiration and guidance from the whales and sea lions. A nice layer of fat is a fabulous invention for keeping one warm, comfortable, and floating gently even in the chilliest of waters.

Looking for a little extra glamour in your Wet-Set wear? While New York and Paris are oohing and aahing over evening dresses with beads and sequins, you can make your grand entrance back onto the boat with a positively sublime wetsuit covered in live krill from head to foot. These precious little creatures, tiny shrimps that will fit a dozen at a time on each of your dainty manicured nails, add a stunning, shimmering shrimp-red accent to any woman's wetsuit.

No outfit can be considered complete without the appropriate accessories. Start with a belt. Big belts are very in this year, and diver's weight belts are guaranteed to fit the bill. Choose hip weights for that oversized chunky look or the more delicate bullet-shaped weights to go with your Che Guevara après-dive t-shirt.

Are you tired of spending your hard-earned money on $20-per-pair nylon panty hose that run the first time you touch them? Trade them in for a pair of neoprene booties. These delicate little beauties are virtually indestructible, and almost as comfortable as your favorite pair of bunny slippers. Or for tropical diving, a pair or two of brightly colored Lycra socks will not only keep you looking stylish but also protect that gorgeous pedicure.

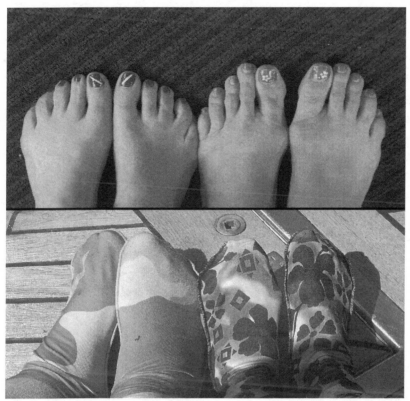

Foot Fashion for the Wet-Set   Solomon Islands (Top Photo)/Sulawesi Island, Indonesia (Bottom Photo)
Judith Hemenway Photo ©

Do you love all that glittery costume jewelry that gleams from every department store jewelry counter? Be a trendsetter and accessorize your outfit with the definitive bling-bling of a chromed regulator. Need to mark your status with the latest in electronic gadgets? The diving industry offers you a sumptuous assortment of dive computers, gauges, and even your own personal underwater GPS navigation device.

Although, sadly, ladies hats have all but disappeared from the fashion scene, trendsetters such as heiress Liz Goldwin consider a proper chapeau to be an essential part of their beauty secret. For divers, you can never go wrong with a neoprene hood. These mahvelous little chapeaux come in two styles: the sporty short-necked warm-water version, reminiscent of the snug-fitting cloches of the Roaring Twenties; and the ever popular cold-water style with its long floppy collar that hints of those romantic wide-brimmed portrait hats à la Audrey Hepburn.

Don't feel completely dressed until you've got your Maui Jim or Juicy Couture sunglasses on? Try a scuba mask instead. With the differential diffraction of light through water compared with air, the mask acts as a pair of reading glasses underwater. An added benefit is that the fishbowl effect makes your eyes look huge and will really accentuate your eye makeup while you are underwater. And if perchance your mask happens to flood? Not to worry. A silly little accident like that will only serve to convert your eyes to the latest in black-eyed-blob fashion.

And don't forget that accessory of all accessories—the handbag. Oversized bags are very stylish this year, and our well-outfitted Glamazon Diving Goddess will be sporting a gear bag that makes those oversized handbags look like teensy little change purses by comparison—and these honeys come all tricked out with buckles, straps, studs, and more compartments than you can imagine.

Have you been spending hours staring into the mirror in your bathroom, practicing expressions that will make your lips look as luscious and pouty as all those lipstick models? No need for collagen injections. Just wrap your lips around the mouthpiece of a scuba regulator, and I guarantee that you will out-pout the best of those models!

Have you been agonizing over the latest slicked-back or wild and whimsical hairstyles in *Modern Salon* or on the fashion runways? Well, girlfriend, there's not a stylist alive who can begin to approach the fabulous fright wig look of your own hairdo, fresh from a therapeutic soak in mineral-rich seawater, as you playfully pull off your neoprene hood and give your fabulous locks a sophisticated après-dive shake.

For those romantic evenings on board the boat, while the North Wind sends its gentle icy zephyrs across the deck, cozy up in the bohemian elegance and luxury of a hooded heavy-duty nylon diver's windbreaker with moisture-wicking fleece lining that is considerably more politically correct than any nasty ole mink coat—and it's washable to boot.

And last, but not least, are you tired of spending 20 bucks a pop to get your fingernails done, only to have them split and chip the moment you leave the salon? Well, ladies, diving is the perfect excuse.

The moment you begin putting on your wetsuit, your nails will start bending and breaking off—so just cut them short to begin with. Diving is the best, most glamorous excuse you can possibly have for going no-nonsense naked with your fingernails.

At the end of our second day of diving, as I took off my wetsuit and booties, I noticed that the precious layers of polish on my toenails were badly chipped and half worn off. Ah well, I'll give up my manicures for diving, but I'll never give up the luxury of those wonderful pedicures. I was back at the salon the next day for another round of pampering and a fresh coat of polish. Let's see . . . what color shall I choose this time? *Rock-apulco Red* or *Malaysian Mist*? Ah! There's the one. *Dancing in the Isles*!

CHAPTER 17

Dolphin Foibles

Paul

I love dolphins; who doesn't? I have never had the privilege of an underwater encounter with free, wild dolphins. That still remains on my bucket list. However, here are two encounters I have had with captive dolphins.

A Dolphin Honeymoon

The year was 1974. Carol and I were honeymooning in the Bahamas. After an uneventful flight from New York's JFK airport, our Pan Am Boeing 727 descended out of puffy, white cumulus clouds as we approached Nassau. This was our first trip to the land of calypso, steel drums, and conch chowder. I was astounded by the ocean's colors as we flew low over the water. Azure blues and aqua-greens melted into each other, producing hues which I thought existed only in retouched travel posters.

Our travel agent had booked us into the Nassau Beach Hotel on Cable Beach. Daytime, we enjoyed basking on the white sand beach and snorkeling in warm, gin-clear water. Nighttime was especially delightful. After dinner, we strolled along the beach, where warm tropical breezes caressed us under a black velvet sky, lit by a silvery moon. Very romantic, indeed!

One evening, we decided to visit Paradise Island for a dinner show and try our luck at the famous casino where James Bond foiled the evil Emilio Largo and charmed the lovely Domino in *Thunderball*. We grabbed a taxi from our hotel to downtown Nassau and a water taxi to Paradise Island. At that time, Nassau and Paradise Island were not as developed as they are now. The casino complex consisted of two hotels, the Britannia Beach and the Loew's Paradise Island Hotel with the casino nestled between them.

Early for the dinner show, we decided to explore the tropical paradise. The beautifully landscaped grounds included lagoon pools, footbridges, palm trees, and native vegetation. Walking hand in hand, we came to a small dock where a wet towel was draped over a wooden railing. Curious, I walked over and picked up the towel while Carol strolled away to examine some colorful flowers and explore other parts of the lagoon.

I heard a strange squawking sound just below my feet. I looked down and saw two dolphins in the water. Real live dolphins! I loved dolphins, but I had never seen one up close and personal. My only contact with these magnificent creatures had been limited to watching reruns of *Flipper*, still a very popular television show in the mid '70s. I was ecstatic, even though these dolphins were captive residents.

The dolphins saw me holding the towel and squawked louder. Being a clever human, I figured out the wet towel was their toy and they were telling me they wanted to play. I held a corner of the towel in my hand and let the other end dangle in the water. Immediately, the dolphins passed under and around the towel, letting it rub against their backs. Wow! Forget TV. I was playing with two Flippers!

I shouted, "Hey Carol, look at this! Come over and see this! Dolphins!"

My attention was diverted. I didn't notice the different sensation transmitted through the towel—a slight tugging. I turned to look. To my amazement, one of the dolphins had turned over on his back and passed back and forth under the wet, rough, terry cloth towel, letting it rub his sensitive area to stimulate his "manhood" until he was fully aroused. Flipper now sported a huge erection! "Pink Floyd," I have since learned, is the non-scientific anatomical term for cetacean displays of sexual prowess, was displayed in all its glory. You've seen how dolphins always appear to have a perpetual smile? Well, this naughty boy appeared overjoyed! The other dolphin watched with seeming approval. I assumed Mrs. Flipper hoped for an interesting evening later on. Perhaps they were also on their honeymoon?

Well, when *my* Mrs. came over and saw the action she was, how shall I say, horrified? Mortified? Shocked? The look in her saucer-wide eyes said it all. I could see my bride, from a conservative, Italian-American Brooklyn family, thinking, *My mother warned me it was a mistake to marry this guy!* But when the initial shock wore off, her expression changed to puzzled interest. Watching Flipper, Carol seemed, well, very impressed. Hell, *I* was impressed, perhaps even a bit envious!

"Stop it right now!" she insisted.

"But honey, he . . . he's not finished," was my lame reply, the only excuse I could conjure up on short notice. But truthfully, I really didn't know what to do. Conflicting thoughts raced through my brain. *Maybe I should stop. But, if I stop, is that cruelty to animals?* I mean, hey, I'm a guy; I can relate to his situation.

"What if someone sees you?" Carol asked.

I hadn't thought of that. We were in a foreign country, and I had no idea what the ramifications could be. But ramifications of what? What exactly would this be considered? Molesting the local wildlife? I had to make a quick decision. I looked down at poor Flipper. He still wasn't finished, but I knew we had to leave. Reluctantly, I pulled up the towel and draped it over the railing where I had found it. Immediately, his angry squawking began. *Well big fella, someone else will be along soon,* I rationalized. *Maybe they'll see the towel and . . .*

After an entertaining Bahamian dinner show and a financially unsuccessful foray at blackjack, we took a casual, moonlit stroll to the pier where the water taxi would take us on the five-minute trip from Paradise Island back to Nassau. I looked back at the lagoon and reflected on my dolphin encounter. I wondered how the rest of

Flipper's evening went. Then I thought about all the hundreds of millions of dollars being spent by scientists and governments to establish communication and connections with non-human species, terrestrial as well as extra-terrestrial. I know I could help them. *First, get a rough terry cloth towel. Next, . . .*

Dolphin Pranks and Cranks

The morning was warm and sunny. I had returned to San Diego, California, the night before from my adventures visiting the gray whales in Mexico's San Ignacio and Scammon's Lagoons (Chapter 19).

My flight back to New York's JFK airport was not until 9:00 p.m., and I had arranged to have dinner with a friend. In the meantime, I had the day to kill, so I decided to take a cab to SeaWorld and see what the free whales' captive cousins were up to.

I wandered over to the dolphin tank, a large enclosure that housed about 20 dolphins. I was reading a map of SeaWorld's attractions when I heard spectators a short distance away scream as a dolphin somehow managed to splash the entire crowd packed along the railing. I watched the people retreat, dripping wet, even several rows back from the railing. I shook my head and wondered how that could have happened. After the crowd thinned out, I walked over to the railing to get a good look at the dolphins. They seemed happy enough, cavorting with each other. But in the wild, they would roam the oceans freely, socialize among their pods, organize hunts for their meals, and use all their natural capabilities to their fullest capacity to survive. I wondered what these intelligent creatures did to keep from going stir-crazy in captivity.

Two dolphins approached the railing and faced a new crowd of unwary spectators. They inched closer and encouraged people eager to approach for a touch. The dolphins would back off and then close in again, pulling more people closer. They backed away one last time and hung together. I heard them click and squeal to each other in their form of communication. Then one dolphin departed while the other one came forward again. The gullible crowd squeezed closer for a touch. As everyone focused on this single dolphin, his partner suddenly appeared, swimming rapidly on her side. With a powerful swipe of her tail fluke, she threw a spray of water over the crowd. Everyone was drenched, including me.

Cameras and clothes soaked with saltwater, we retreated to the restrooms to get towels and dry off. Later, I stood a safe distance from the dolphin tank and watched these two dolphins switch roles as decoy and splasher and prank another unsuspecting group. Clearly, they had devised this plan on their own for their amusement. They would sucker the gullible humans close, and when they had attracted a sufficiently large crowd, one dolphin acted as the decoy while the partner circled and returned to drench their victims. I could not determine if the dolphins' intent was malicious or prankish, but it was definitely mischievously intelligent, as if they were saying, *Fluke you!*

Several minutes later, another encounter gave me pause for thought. I passed a quiet section of this large tank, where a solitary dolphin floated on the surface within arm's reach. We looked at each other for a minute, and I extended my hand to stroke the dolphin. Usually, if an animal does not wish to be touched, it will back away. I waited for a reaction, but the dolphin remained motionless. I reached out, careful to avoid the blowhole and eyes, and gently touched the sensitive melon, the large curved part of the forehead dolphins use for echolocation. Without warning, the dolphin swung its rostrum, the hard beak, upward, striking the fleshy part of my palm just below the thumb. The blow was so hard and violent, it felt like someone struck my hand with a hammer.

Naturally, I withdrew my sore hand while the dolphin remained where it was. There was no mistaking the dolphin's intent. This was not a playful gesture, but a sharp rebuke. Perhaps the dolphin was having a bad day or angry at being held captive. Perhaps it was annoyed that I had touched a sensitive area. Who knows? But I had a strong feeling that if the dolphin had a choice, it would have preferred to cruise the Pacific with its pod and chase speedy jacks or other baitfish for lunch, rather than being displayed in a cement tank for human amusement.

After snorkeling with free whales and diving with other marine creatures, I have developed mixed feelings about whether we should keep large marine mammals in captivity. The arguments cut both ways. Some people are strongly against captive programs because they believe these mammals should remain free to roam the oceans, not held in an unnatural, constrictive environment. Scientists report captive whales and dolphins exhibit psychologically aberrant behavior after years in captivity. Many organizations, SeaWorld included, now breed marine mammals in captivity instead of capturing wild individuals. Given that these are intelligent animals, I often wonder what a mother dolphin or whale (orcas and other small whales that can tolerate captive environments such as pilot whales and belugas) would communicate to her offspring. I suspect the "conversation" would be quite different, depending if she was captured as a free whale or bred in captivity.

However, some people are in favor of captivity programs because it allows the public to see animals they would likely never encounter, gain an appreciation for them, and become their public advocates. Hopefully, the knowledge gained by scientists and caretakers would contribute in some way to the survival of the species in the wild.

I have swung in favor of the freedom argument, especially in light of recent studies that indicate these highly intelligent creatures have a sense of "self" and a personal identity, which they exhibit by using unique call signs, the equivalent of a name. This also raises the question of how several generations of breeding would affect such an intelligent being. Because of past difficulties in releasing marine mammals back into the wild, it seems that already-captive dolphins and whales will have to remain in a captive environment. For example, Keiko, aka Free Willy, was released but never fully integrated with orca whale society despite attempts to acclimate him to the wild. He succumbed 16 months after his release.

An interesting compromise has arisen in some areas. Resorts in Roatan and Turks and Caicos feature semi-captive programs. Divers can interact with dolphins that are allowed to leave their "home facility" and follow the dive boat into the open ocean, and then return with the boat to the facility. Given that these dolphins freely choose to return raises some interesting questions. If a dolphin voluntarily chooses to return to a semi-captive environment, should we consider the dolphin a captive or a free dolphin? Is there a different ethical standard for a program that gives dolphins a choice? If dolphins have the capacity to choose safety and free food over a totally free environment, what does that imply about their capacity for intelligence and self-awareness, etc.?

In May 2014, India's Ministry of Environment and Forests gave dolphins the status of "Non-Human Persons" and declared killing a dolphin as murder. The declaration also forbids keeping dolphins captive anywhere in the country and bans dolphin shows. That is an interesting alternative to Japan, which permits the slaughter and capture of dolphins in their infamous Taiji Cove.

Hopefully other countries will follow India's lead.

CHAPTER 18

STALKING THE WILY WHATEVER

Judy

In the early days, scuba diving (like most, if not all, sports) was the domain of men. These "manly men" battled man-eating sharks and stalked great game fishes. Nothing else that lived in the ocean mattered. Today, the Women Divers Hall of Fame (http://www.wdhof.org) boasts 186 members, sharks are viewed more as fascinating and increasingly threatened creatures, and most scuba divers hunt with cameras rather than spearguns. The Solomon Islands provides prime hunting territory for shutterbugs such as Jon and me, who have twice had the great pleasure of living aboard and diving from the *M. V. Bilikiki*, one of the best dive boats anywhere in the world.

Crooked Point, Kovahika Island, Solomons, Sunday August 15, 2004. Olga spotted it first, and she showed it to Monty, who then showed it to Heidi, who showed it to Eric. As I dropped down to join the others, Eric motioned me to join him, pointing to a particular area of a three-foot-wide, delicate pink fan coral. I knew instantly what he was pointing at, and I could barely contain my excitement as I moved in, slowly and carefully, for a close-up look. I scanned the surface of the fan intently, but even though I knew exactly what I was looking for, it still took me endless seconds to see it. Suddenly, as though my eyes were a radar screen acquiring a target, the image leaped out of its background: a pygmy seahorse (*Hippocampus denise*). What an incredible creature! It was no longer than my pinkie fingernail, and half as wide, with the exact same texture and color as the pink fan it gripped with its tiny, curled tail.

The rush of adrenaline made my hands shake as I maneuvered my camera rig in to take some photos. Three shots later, when the strobes didn't fire, I realized that the film advance wasn't working. I had set it wrong. It was frustrating not to be able to capture my first-ever pygmy, but I was hopeful that I would have other chances in the eight days remaining on this trip.

Five days later, at Twin Points on Mbolu Island in Marovo Lagoon, Michelle found two of them for us, perfectly camouflaged on their pink fan coral homes. Because we were near the end of the dive, at 65 feet, I had only a few minutes to squeeze off a few shots of them before heading up to shallower waters. This time, I had my camera set properly and I successfully captured the little tykes on film—cherished treasures from the beautiful waters of the Solomon Islands.

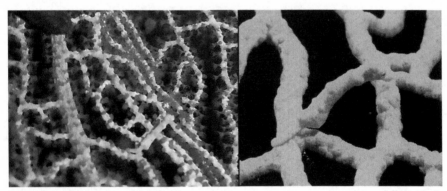

Can You Find the Pygmy Seahorse in Each Photo?   Solomon Islands
Judith Hemenway Photos ©

On the same trip, I had my first encounter with a slightly larger cousin to the pygmy, the ornate (or harlequin) ghost pipefish (*Solenostomus paradoxus*). These pipefish vary considerably in both size and coloration; the one I saw was red and white, less than one and a half inches long. Like the pygmy seahorse, this marvelous creature hung out in a pink sea fan that was only about two shades lighter in color than the pipefish. The decorative white tufts of the pipefish closely mimicked the white polyps of the sea fan. So well disguised are these pipefish that I was unable to spot one on my own, even though I knew which fans to inspect. I had to depend on our guide, Monty, who quickly found one for me. Even with Monty pointing to the right location on the fan, it took my eyes and brain multiple seconds of staring before the pipefish "popped" out of its background and became visible to me.

Recognizing visual patterns is a learned skill, and each pattern must be acquired on its own. Learning to see the pattern of the pygmy seahorse did not help me at all to see the pattern of the ornate ghost pipefish. But it does seem as though, once you've mastered a particular pattern, the time and effort your brain needs to recognize new instances of that pattern decrease significantly.

The Harlequin Ghost Pipefish Is Well-Camouflaged   Solomon Islands
Judith Hemenway Photo ©

Of course, not all sea creatures are as cleverly camouflaged. Nudibranchs, for instance, are known for their outrageously flamboyant colors and patterns. On our second trip to the Solomons, I was

captivated by a photo hanging in the main salon of a dusky (or variable neon) nembrotha (*Nembrotha kubaryana*). With its black body,
neon-green polka-dot markings, and flaming red-orange gills and rhinophores, it looked more like a circus clown than a mollusk. I was
entranced. I absolutely had to see one in the water and get photos of it!

According to our divemasters, Sam and Kellie, our best opportunity would be the wreck of the *Mbike* in the Florida Island Group,
so I was primed and pumped when we arrived at the wreck site. We
went directly down the buoy rope to the wreck and located *Nembrotha
kubaryana* straightaway. Several of them.

Nembrotha kubaryana Would Make a Great Circus Clown   Solomon Islands
Judith Hemenway Photo ©

With their flamboyant color scheme, they're really easy to spot,
although somewhat challenging to photograph, since they tend to stay
tucked under overhangs and similar protected spots, forcing the photographer to go through a variety of contortions to get good shots.
After we took a bunch of photos, we went off to explore more of the
wreck itself. I found a nest of lionfish amidships, near the mast—five

or six in all, tucked into a nook. There was another small one on top, and then a big one floating around, too. I was happily watching these guys when Jon motioned me to a spot on the upper part of the wreck, where I got my best sequence of photos of the nembrotha. Instead of being tucked away down under, this guy strolled around on one of the ship's crossmembers, in the open, as brazen as could be. I shot from a variety of angles. Very exciting!

Turning now to larger (and somewhat threatening) sea critters, we were diving another spot in the Florida Island Group, the Ghavutu Seaplane Base, a World War II site, when Divemaster Kellie spotted something under a large rock ledge. She motioned for us to stop and spread out some distance from the ledge. It was dark under there, but I saw something move as it lurked in the shadows. Kellie picked up some shell fragments and carefully placed them in front of the ledge. She kept herself as far from the ledge as possible and retreated quickly after she dropped the shells. The shadowy creature finally moved far enough to the front of the overhanging rock that I was able to see that it was a peacock mantis shrimp (*Odontodactylus scyllarus*). With its day-glow green-and-blue markings, large bulbous eyes on top of high stalks, and bright orange boxing-glove front legs (with white spots), it looked like the Monster from the Hallucinogenic Lagoon. I understood at once why Kellie was being careful.

Although they are small relative to humans (about eight inches long or less), they have a well-deserved reputation for pugilistic prowess. According to Wikipedia, these guys can punch at a speed of over 50 miles per hour, generating a force of about 200 pounds per hit. They can easily smash a diver's mask or inflict a nasty, bruising punch. I had heard of these formidable creatures and was delighted to finally have the chance to see and photograph one of them. We all waited patiently, cameras at the ready, for him to emerge from his hiding place. Several times, Kellie ventured out to offer more shell fragments, until finally his curiosity (or bellicosity) got the better of him and he emerged briefly into the open. I was able to get one good shot of him before he once more retreated to his lair.

Peacock Mantis Shrimp: The Monster from the Hallucinogenic Lagoon   Solomon Islands
Judith Hemenway Photo ©

While many times our knowledgeable divemasters have been able to take us to known hangouts for specific critters, there are frequent encounters that are serendipitous and provide unanticipated delights, such as the time we returned to the boat across a sand flat.

Sand flats can be pretty boring and devoid of life, but on this particular day, we encountered two juvenile goldenfinned triggerfish, duking it out over a single hidey-hole. As we watched, one of them dived into the hole headfirst, but the other one was not about to give up such a prime piece of real estate. Without hesitation, he charged over, grabbed the claim-jumper by the tail, and with a triumphant flourish, pulled it back out!

Another serendipitous instance was the dive on which we hunted for mandarinfish but didn't find any. I was somewhat glumly working my way back to the boat when I spotted some pajama cardinalfish (*Sphaeramia nematoptera*), which I had never seen before.

They are small fish, with chrome yellow heads, huge red eyes, a big black vertical stripe down their midsection, and behind that, a white tail-end with red polka dots. Seriously!

Pajama Cardinalfish   Solomon Islands
Judith Hemenway Photo ©

They were so wildly strange, I couldn't help but laugh as I took their pictures. While I chuckled and shot, Debbie swam over and motioned for me to follow her. On the far side of a small outcropping of rocks, she pointed to another fish I had never seen before. These were juvenile harlequin sweetlips (*Plectorhinchus chaetodonoides*).

Although the adults of this species are a fairly mundane cream color with brown spots, the juveniles are a reddish-brown, with a few outsized white spots and white fins and tails that are at least two sizes too large for the tiny fish. They flippy-flop up and down and around, looking for all the world like a puppy that trips over its own feet or an overgrown, spastic, hyperactive butterfly.

I followed several of them around and tried desperately to capture their images with my camera. But their movements were too rapid and unpredictable for still photos, especially when the photographer was almost doubled over, laughing hysterically at the show. Finally I came to my senses, switched my camera over to video mode, and managed to get several good clips of a medium-sized juvenile and then a much smaller one. I still laugh every time I view these clips:

You can view both these juveniles on YouTube:
http://tinyurl.com/itty-bitty-flippy
http://tinyurl.com/bigger-floppy-floppy

And then there are the occasional real mysteries, the critters no one has ever seen before, that can't be found in any of the many reference books in the boat's library. One lovely tranquil morning before dawn, I leaned on the side railing, gazing out at the dark ocean and darker islands that gradually emerged in the predawn light. I looked down into the water around the boat and saw dozens and dozens of tiny neon-blue dots adrift in the water. Though most of them appeared to float passively, it was clear that some of them were actively swimming. We kept our eyes on them through breakfast, and then captured several in a paper cup.

What strange creatures! If left alone, they would show their iridescent blue, but if disturbed, they disappeared, and it was extremely hard to get a good look at them. They looked like tiny crustaceans, about a quarter-inch long or less, with a rounded front, blunt rear, and possibly three main body segments. Their bodies were very flat, with cilia or legs underneath. They're definitely bioluminescent—they could turn that blue on and off, and flash it either front to back, or back to front, or just back, etc.

After we returned home, I did some web surfing to see if I could identify these creatures, and my best guess is that they are isopods (an order of crustaceans), perhaps *Cirolana diminuta* or *Cirolana harfordi*.

I could go on and on, telling stories of the many strange and marvelous creatures I have seen in almost 40 years of diving. Scientists have catalogued over 1.2 million species of living things that inhabit the earth, with almost 200,000 of those being marine species. But that is only the species we know about! Furthermore, the western South Pacific area is one of the most remarkable regions of the world, both with respect to number of species (biodiversity) and sheer numbers of organisms (biomass). It's no wonder that every time I go diving there, I experience the phenomenon I described in my trip journal on Tuesday August 17, 2004:

> *I'm definitely on sensory overload at this point. The days and dives swirl around me like a psychedelic oil slick, each experience merging with the others and not enough time to absorb them. At night when I close my eyes, the reefs in my visions reel and pulse in the darkness like a living kaleidoscope.*

On the first few dives of every trip, I eagerly try to look at everything and identify it by name, but the overwhelming numbers and variety rapidly outstrip my cognitive capabilities. At that point, I go dumb and retreat into an awestruck pre-verbal mode of being, content to immerse myself in the glories and wonders of this incredible liquid world.

CHAPTER 19

THE FRIENDLY GRAY WHALES OF BAJA

Paul

To Touch a Wild Whale

Glancing at the ocean's surface from a beach or skimming over the waves on a boat often makes me wonder about inhabitants below and their daily struggle to survive. I think about past experiences and future adventures, and I cannot wait to dive in and explore. If the day included an unexpected visit from passing dolphins or a surprise breach from a humpback whale, I reflected on close encounters in Tonga and the Dominican Republic's Silver Bank. Then I would let my mind wander and think about what it would be like, not just to encounter a whale but to actually touch a whale.

This unlikely adventure began with an e-mail invitation from Judy, similar to our whale snorkeling adventure in Tonga (see Chapter 11).

> Hey Paul,
>
> Jon and I are going to Baja to meet the friendly gray whales.
> Care to join us?
>
> Judy

I had wanted to make this trip for many years, ever since I watched a National Geographic television special about the friendly whales of San Ignacio Lagoon. The episode featured mother whales bringing their newborn calves for close encounters with boatloads of tourists. I watched, mesmerized, as the whales approached the small boats for TLC from whale lovers, and I resolved to visit San Ignacio Lagoon—someday.

A couple of years after watching that National Geographic special, Carol and I drove to Montauk for a short vacation and lobster dinner at the famous Gosman's Dock restaurant. On the way, I stopped at Book Hampton, a great local independent book shop in East Hampton. *The Eye of the Whale,* by Dick Russell caught my eye. Russell documented gray whale behavior and their amazing encounters with humans. Russell's book and photos strengthened my resolve to travel to Baja and meet the whales. Of course, "life" usually gets in the way and disrupts most plans. Sometimes you just need a catalyst. My catalyst was spelled J-U-D-Y.

Sure, I replied to Judy's e-mail. *Send me the details.* Several months later in March, I boarded a flight from snowy, slushy JFK airport, headed for sunny San Diego. Judy and Jon met me later that afternoon at the local Marriott, and we headed back to their place for dinner to discuss logistics and meet their longtime friends Tom, Molly, Brooke, and Kristen, who were also making the trek.

The next morning, we departed for the airport where we would meet our bus and the tour group. I was the only loner in the bunch. Almost everyone else was a couple, but my other half was back in Long Island, New York. When Carol read the itinerary—hours riding in small boats in choppy water . . . long van rides over unpaved roads— she begged off the trip.

We took our seats and departed for a 5-day 435-mile bus ride halfway down Mexico's Baja Peninsula and back. Our Andiamo tour guide, Karla, informed us that the Baja Peninsula was longer than Italy. As we motored south, Karla kept us informed about the ever-changing environment, regional differences, local fauna and customs, and other interesting facts. We were also accompanied by Rebekah Bohm, a guide from the Scripps/Birch Aquarium. During the bus ride, Rebekah gave us a mini-course about gray whale biology, their behavior, and habits.

After two days, we arrived at the sleepy little town of San Ignacio, where gray whale murals adorned almost every wall. I assumed the town was right next to the lagoon. Never having been a Boy Scout, I really should have taken a map-reading course. Someone, probably an ex-Boy Scout, pointed out that San Ignacio sits in the middle of Baja, equidistant from the Sea of Cortez on one side and the Pacific on the other. To reach the whales, we would have to take a three-hour ride, not in our comfortable tour bus but in a convoy of three airport-type vans.

The next morning after breakfast, we set out for the lagoon, bouncing over an unpaved, bumpy desert road at 15 to 20 miles per hour. Of the 22 people in our group, only 4 or 5 were under 40. The rest, including me, were 60+, several were in their 70s. At least 1 or 2 were spry 80-year-olds. Ages aside, this was indeed a hardy group of adventurers, and there were no stragglers for the entire week. However, we did have to stop every hour to water the cacti. I prayed, *Kidneys, don't fail me now!*

Almost three grueling hours later, we finally reached San Ignacio Lagoon. We piled out of our vans, eager to venture out onto the water and meet the whales. We ate a light lunch and received a short orientation about gray whale encounters. Then our group scrambled into three pangas, small motorized fishing boats, each with a single driver who steered and operated the outboard. Our "Gang of Seven" (Jon, Judy, Tom, Molly, Brooke, Kristen, and me) had a boat to ourselves. Our driver was a local named Luis. Before heading out, we donned flotation jackets.

Luis explained why. "The whales occasionally use our small boats as back scratchers, and accidents sometimes happen. If we capsize, we don't want to lose anyone."

Soon, the seven of us floated in the middle of San Ignacio Lagoon in Baja, Mexico, surrounded by dozens of California gray whales. We shouted every time we saw a whale breach, exploding from below the surface like a submarine-launched missile. Other whales crossed our bow or stern alone or in pairs, some accompanied by their newborn calves. We leaned over the side and splashed the water with our hands to attract their babies' curiosity and hoped for a close encounter.

It was a 15-minute ride out to the deeper parts of the lagoon, where the whales hung out. Soon we saw a whale spyhop. It appeared to stand on its tail flukes for several seconds as it elevated about one-third of its body out of the water to observe its surroundings, before sinking back underwater. We saw blows all around us, several hundred yards away, almost too many to count.

"Let's get closer!" several of us shouted. A gray whale's misty exhalation formed a distinct heart-shape pattern before dissolving in the air.

Luis cut the motor and we drifted, hoping a curious whale would find us sufficiently interesting for a close encounter. Whales continually crossed our bow, stern, and occasionally kept pace with us, close enough to spray us with their steamy breath, but keeping out of arm's reach. We noticed that one large adult whale had a huge chunk of meat missing from its back. The exposed white blubber starkly contrasted with its dark-gray, mottled color where the skin was unbroken.

"That injury is probably from a killer whale attack," someone said.

Orcas are known to attack the grays during their long migrations between Alaska and the Baja. They frequently harass and distract the adults so they can kill the baby whales.

Gray whales appear different from other whale species in several ways. Lacking a true dorsal fin, their spine resembles the knuckles of your hand when you make a fist. Their pectoral fins are not long and graceful like a humpback, but short and stubby. Their skin is not smooth like a finback or a blue whale, but covered with barnacles and patches of sea lice, probably their most distinctive, unglamorous feature.

We had cruised around the lagoon for a couple of hours now, disappointed that we had not yet experienced a close encounter. At least it was a calm, sunny day, so no one needed to "feed the fish" to relieve seasickness. Luis looked at his watch and contacted the other pangas on his walkie-talkie more frequently than before. We realized from his body language that he wanted to return to shore, but we still had not experienced our magical moment. These whales seemed a bit standoffish. Very few were accompanied by newborns. We decided that this area of the lagoon was probably not the nursery but the hangout for the teenagers and young adults. Like other healthy young mammals, they probably had other activities on their minds rather than associating with the tourists.

Luis turned the boat and began slowly making his way toward shore, when our patience was rewarded. A mother gray and her calf turned and approached our panga. I noticed that the baby's skin was more black than gray and smooth, free of barnacles and sea lice it would acquire later in life. Luis cut the motor once again, and we drifted, splashing the water with our hands, hoping to entice the whales closer.

"Come on Mama, come on Baby," I heard Judy and Molly shout, encouraging the whales to come toward our boat. We saw the baby whale sink below the surface with barely a ripple, while Mom floated several feet away, watching us. I had decided to sit near the stern, the lowest part of the boat near the water, so I could dip my waterproof camera below the surface and get some underwater shots. However, I found that this algae-laden water was too green and murky for clear shots, so my plan was stymied. I sat with the camera in my lap and watched Mom, wondering where Baby had gone.

I noticed the water ripple next to where I sat and looked down. Without warning, the baby whale surfaced right next to me. The big moment had arrived, but I was startled into paralysis. Someone up front snapped me out of my trance, shouting, "Look! The whale's next to you! Go for it!"

I reached down and touched the baby whale's head. Its skin was soft and smooth, similar to a wet inner tube, but with bone just beneath the skin it felt firm and hard. My touch startled the baby whale. It froze for a moment, then, perhaps curiosity satisfied, it gently sank below the boat. I watched as the water closed over its head. Seconds later, Baby surfaced next to Mom. The magic moment happened so quickly that I never had time to snap a photo. We remained for a few more minutes hoping the whales would grant someone else a touch, but they soon moved away. Luis revved the motor, and we headed for shore.

"Did you touch it?" someone asked.

I grinned and nodded. My boat mates were genuinely happy for me. "All right!"

"Oh, you are so lucky!"

I sat quietly in thought on the boat ride back to shore, trying to relive the brief moment. I felt privileged that fate had granted me a unique experience, something few other people have ever enjoyed. When we all met up, the rest of our group from the other pangas roundly congratulated me when they learned I had touched a baby whale. I have often reflected on the significance that a free, wild whale was curious enough to interact with us and let me touch it. The thought has never left me.

The Whales Who Came to Play

After our day and night in San Ignacio, we headed north the next morning to the town of Guerrero Negro and Scammon's Lagoon, named after the famous whaling captain Charles Scammon, who discovered the lagoons and the gray whale population in the 1850s. Scammon's whalers butchered the whales, harpooning baby whales to draw the adults closer for the killing. The whales reacted ferociously as they defended their young, killing whalers by smashing their small wooden whale boats to splinters. Because of their fury and anger, whalers bestowed the moniker devil fish. (An ironic footnote: Scammon ended his days as an anti-whaling conservationist.)

The van ride to Scammon's Lagoon was not as traumatic as the long, bumpy ride to San Ignacio. After 30 minutes over a paved road, we donned our life jackets, dressed to meet the whales. We brimmed with anticipation, optimistically hopeful that we would experience more frequent encounters than we did at San Ignacio.

San Ignacio Lagoon is relatively small and well-protected, so we enjoyed calm conditions as we observed whales cavorting all around us. By contrast, Scammon's Lagoon is much larger than San Ignacio and provided an entirely different experience, both in the mood of the whales and the surrounding environment. The weather was cool and windy, the lagoon choppy. Salty spray doused us as our tiny outboard panga plowed through the waves in search of whales. We huddled low and maintained a heads-down position as we bounced across the waves for a 15-minute high-speed trip to deep water. I doubted we would ever pick out a whale blow through the churning white caps. Fortunately, we moved fast, and no one got seasick. As it turned out, we did not have to strain our eyes searching the horizon for the geyser-like spray of a whale's blow. These whales came to play! They appeared out of nowhere, repeatedly surfacing next to our boat and blowing, covering us in their misty whale breath. Lucky for us, their breath was relatively odorless and did not smell fishy since they were not feeding, However, the mist had an oily consistency, so it smudged when I wiped it from my eyeglasses and camera lens.

Several times, mothers and calves swam alongside, and sometimes passed beneath us, using our panga as a giant backscratcher, just as Luis had warned us yesterday. The water here was much clearer than at San Ignacio, and I was able to lean over the side, extend my arms below the surface, and get some good video of the whales below us. On the video, we could see them beneath our panga swimming upside down, then rolling as they passed under us and surfaced on the other side.

The highlight of the day was a mother and calf encounter. The two whales swam alongside. Our boat driver had to maintain an even speed to keep pace with the whales because this pair had some destination in mind and did not slow down. The baby approached, close enough for Judy and those at the front to lean over to attempt a quick touch.

Our Scripps/Birch Aquarium guide, Rebekah, kept shouting, "So close! Oh, so close!" Mom crossed over her baby and maintained a position between us and the calf. She remained close, less than five feet away. This adult whale was large, easily 40 feet long, with such a massive girth, that the backwash of the water off her body made our tiny panga pitch and roll, dangerously close to tipping over. As I shot video, I reflected that my perspective, holding the camera right next to the whale's midsection, was the same view a nineteenth-century whaler would have had as he raised his harpoon and prepared for the kill. Hearing the whales' forceful exhalations right next to our boat provided a dramatic sense of the powerful life force so close to us.

This short YouTube video clip shows the action:
http://tinyurl.com/friendly-whales

Eventually the two whales pulled away and veered out toward the deeper part of the lagoon. We wished them well and scanned the water for more whales.

We observed parallel grooves on the flukes and pectoral fins of several whales during the day. Rebekah informed us these were scars from killer whale attacks. That reality, contrasting with the whales' playfulness in their relaxed, protected sanctuary, was sobering. Rebekah said an estimated 300 whales are born in these peaceful lagoons every year, but killer whales will take about 100 as the mothers and their calves migrate north along the California coast to their Arctic feeding grounds. Another 100 will die from natural causes. Jon's photograph below graphically illustrates the violence gray whales endure along

Tooth-Scarred Fluke   Baja California Sur, Mexico
Photo Courtesy of Jon Fellows ©

their perilous journey. On this whale's tail fluke, you can clearly see indentations and deep grooves from orca teeth, when the whale pulled free from a killer whale's deadly jaws.

We learned that orcas are not the only obstacle these whales face. Recently, many have died from starvation or appeared emaciated when they reach the lagoons. Their food supply, tiny amphipods, bottom-dwelling crustaceans, is becoming scarce. One reason might be global warming, which could affect the life cycle of the amphipods, and the rest of the whale's food supply—phytoplankton (tiny plants and algae that also help make up plankton), small micro-zooplankton (the division of zooplankton that are smaller than 1/127th of an inch in size), and detritus.

Our visit with the whales was over too quickly. After two hours on the water, we took a quick van ride back to our tour bus and headed north. We enjoyed a last night of eating and partying together, and shared our thoughts about our unique experience. The next morning, we headed toward San Diego. Since we arrived at night, I had a full day before my flight back to New York. I spent the day at SeaWorld communing with whales' captive cousins, the dolphins and orcas (see Chapter 17).

Our New York bound flight took off over San Diego's Mission Bay and the Pacific before turning east. I looked down at the sea, hoping to see the wake of massive bodies moving through the sea or spot some blows, but the water appeared calm and clear. I knew that the friendly grays we had encountered would soon leave the safety of their peaceful lagoons and traverse these dangerous waters toward their Alaskan feeding grounds. I reflected on the orca-teeth scars I had seen on the adult whales, veterans of the passage. Then, I thought about the baby gray whale I had touched. I hoped that calf and his mother would safely survive the killer whale gauntlet that awaited them on their journey north.

CHAPTER 20

OCEAN SONGS AND WHISPERS

Judy

One of the crew members on our boat was wearing a bright royal blue shirt that read, "Azul Profundo." (Profound or deep blue.) That phrase stuck with me as Jon and I stepped off the swim step into the warm, clear blue Caribbean water. We were diving Eagle's Nest, a spot off the east coast of South Caicos Island. We headed east, away from the island, finning slowly, leisurely, as we enjoyed the corals and fish and other sea life. We followed the ocean bottom as it sloped eastward gradually down to a steep drop-off at about 80 feet, beyond which only azul profundo existed. I knew if we headed eastward into that deep blue, we would have to cross a 25-mile-wide deep ocean channel before we reached land again, the island of Grand Turk. Of course, that was a little beyond our dive plan.

As we meandered along toward the drop-off, something nagged at the edges of my awareness, and then suddenly I realized what it was—whale song! Somewhere nearby, a humpback whale was singing. I looked around briefly for the singer but quickly realized that he wasn't within visual range. I returned to my slow meander. But now my attention was only half-heartedly focused on what I saw. Most of me was utterly entranced by what I heard. Of course, I had heard recordings of humpback whale songs, but never live, in the water. It's as though I were swimming through a liquid song, suspended in the melody.

When I reached the drop-off, I stopped and hovered, hanging there, enthralled by the haunting, mysterious, otherworldly sound, until Jon tapped me gently on the shoulder and pointed into the deep blue beyond. There was the singer himself, lazily gliding along the edge, about 30 feet out and at the same depth as us. He cruised past in slow motion, singing his song, completely unconcerned by our presence.

After the dive, Jon and I compared notes. We agreed it was like watching an Aikido Master, but the images we had fixed in our minds were wildly different. My image was that of relaxed grace and effortless economy of movement, with not a single microjoule of energy wasted, while Jon's image was that of immense power and single-minded speed.

Both images are fitting, and neither of them adequately and completely captures what we had seen. Every time I have had the privilege of hearing these otherworldly songs while diving, I am captivated, both by the songs themselves, and by the knowledge that there are other beings, besides humans, with the urge and the creativity to craft such songs.

Over the past several decades, as researchers have investigated and publicized their findings, humpbacks and their songs have captured the imagination of humans around the world. Dr. Roger Payne, one of the foremost experts on humpback songs, says that these songs are typically 5 to 15 minutes long, but can range up to 30 minutes and may be repeated without any break in between for as long as 36 hours. Each song consists of anywhere from 2 to 9 themes, and each theme includes phrases that are repeated 15 to 20 times. Every group of whales has its own distinct song that all singers in the group sing, and the song evolves over time, again, with every member of the group incorporating the changes that are introduced.

While humpbacks are the only cetaceans that produce such highly sophisticated songs, it is clear that the other cetaceans, both the baleen and the toothed whales and dolphins, use sound for a variety of purposes, including communication and echolocation. In addition to these two purposes, bottlenose dolphins also produce signature whistles that act as unique individual identifiers. In effect, each dolphin invents its own name!

The Ship's Hull Vibrates with Whale Song   Tonga, South Pacific
Judith Hemenway Photo ©

Sperm whales produce the loudest sounds of any animal on earth, and blue whales produce the lowest-pitched sounds. Blue whale sounds are so low-pitched that they are often inaudible to humans, who may instead experience the sounds as felt vibrations. Blue whale communications are so effective that one whale can hear another as far away as 2,500 miles (the distance between California and Hawaii).

While I have never had the opportunity to hear other cetacean sounds while diving, the ocean is filled with an immense variety of sounds that are an integral component of every diving experience. The one sound above all others, omnipresent on every dive, is the sound of one's own breathing. On land, unless one is exercising heavily, breathing is a silent act. Air is everywhere around us, and our breathing is controlled by our subconscious, autonomic nervous system, so there is no need to even think about it.

Scuba diving, however, is another situation entirely. We must carry our air with us in tanks on our backs, and our supply is severely limited. In cold waters, at depths of 80 or 100 feet, a tank of air may last only a half-hour or so. In warm shallow waters, if I am not exerting myself, I can personally manage to stretch a tank of air out to maybe two hours—still a very short period of time. Breathing becomes an act of much greater significance, and the sound of one's own breathing—the Darth Vader-like inhalation, and the bubbling, gurgling exhalation—become reassuring sounds that one's tank and regulator are working properly, God's in His heaven, and all's right with the world.

Similarly, if diving from a boat, the hum of the boat's generator provides reassurance that home is close at hand. In contrast, the buzz of an outboard motor directly overhead like a monstrous mosquito when one is ascending (usually low on air) toward the surface at the end of a dive is definitely an alarm trigger!

If you reach beyond the sound of your own breathing, beyond the sounds of human-made generators and engines, you can hear the constant background sounds of the ocean itself. Like a quiet summer evening in the country, with its crickets and frogs and the wind whispering in the trees, the ocean, too, has its native chorus: the faint but incessant crackle of snapping shrimp, which seems to be the basic "white noise" of the ocean reefs; the staccato crunches of parrotfish as they munch on coral; the soft whoosh of surf as it curls and breaks overhead, and even the occasional muted clunk of rocks as the surge pushes them against each other.

Once while I was snorkeling in Morovo Lagoon off of Wickham Island, I noticed in one shallow sandy area that the wave action caused the broken shells and sand to tinkle like hundreds of tiny wind chimes. For a while, I stopped and listened as I floated, drifting to and fro on the waves. I had never imagined that sand could sing.

A few days earlier on the same trip, at Karumolun Point in the Russells, I had stumbled upon a fairly large feisty anemonefish. She rose far off her anemone to patrol her territory. (With anemonefish, the large ones are the females and the smaller ones the males.) Much to my surprise, I could actually hear her snapping audibly at me.

I heard a parrotfish for the first time on the tiny island of Sipadan off the northeast coast of Borneo. It was hot that afternoon, so the cooling effects of our after-lunch dive didn't last very long, and our little thatched-roof hut wasn't much cooler than the sun-fried beach. To cool off, we decided to go for a midafternoon snorkel. Sipadan was an ideal place for both diving and snorkeling.

A Bleeker's Parrotfish Crunches Coral   Sulawesi Island, Indonesia
Judith Hemenway Photo ©

Because it is nothing more than the jungle-crowned top of an under-water pinnacle, the beach slope continues without break from the edge of the jungle (where the huts are situated) out about 30–40 feet into the water before plunging precipitously straight down a 2,000-foot drop-off. The walls of the drop-off allow you to pick your depth for diving and provide spectacular scenery along every square foot. For snorkeling, the shallows above the drop-off are pocked with scattered rocks and small clumps of coral, perfect for leisurely floating and sightseeing.

Near the end of our excursion, as we came back around the pier toward the huts, we stumbled upon a veritable army of parrotfish, all busily munching on the chunks of coral strewn about.

The sound of their activity is quite audible, even from 40 or 50 feet away. So named because their teeth form a hard, bird-like beak, the parrotfish use their beaks to pulverize the coral, gleaning from it the nutrition of the coral polyps and possibly the algae that make their homes with the coral animals.

I watched and listened in astonishment as these fish fed on the rock-hard coral heads, and I realized that in the process of eating the coral, they were rapidly and efficiently producing new sand, streams of which spurted from their underbellies periodically as they fed!

The next morning on our first dive of the day, we experienced quite a different sound, which thankfully we have never heard since. We were diving at Turtle Patch, one of the many lovely spots along the drop-off surrounding the island. As usual, we saw a number of turtles (for which Sipadan is renowned). As we drifted along, there was one spot where we were able to swim among a cloud of yellow and white butterflies, along with schools of yellows and other darker fish, all of them only 5–6 inches long. It felt like floating in Wonderland. As we worked our way along the wall, we heard a series of three very loud explosions that really scared me. I had no idea what it was, but I had visions of a gunboat overhead dropping depth charges on us. We felt, more than heard the sounds, as concussions on our chests.

After we surfaced, Divemaster Haris explained that it was probably the sound of the natives dynamiting fish on the next island, which was 10 miles away! Dynamiting was, at that time, a very popular method for fishing.

The natives mix powdered sugar and fertilizer, both of which are readily available, to form an explosive. The mixture is apparently pretty volatile and unpredictable, resulting in frequent injuries, but they continued to use it because it stuns large numbers of fish that can then be gathered easily off the surface.

Haris confirmed that such explosives had been used occasionally on Sipadan before the dive camp was established, which explained the areas of reef we had seen that were nothing but piles of broken-up, dead coral rubble.

Over the 20 years since we experienced those explosions, worldwide awareness of the devastation caused by such fishing practices has increased significantly, and a great deal of effort has been focused on developing and adopting fishing techniques that do not cause such extensive "by-catch" and damage. Hopefully, that means divers will never again hear such explosions.

In contrast to those sounds of destruction, on our most recent trip on the *M. V. Bilikiki* to the Solomon Islands, we were fortunate enough to hear something quite rare and remarkable. We were diving Mborokua Island, a tiny island about 20 miles west of the Russell Island group and 40 miles east-southeast of Marovo Lagoon. Sometimes called Mary's Island, or Murray Island, this gem offers clear water and a magical spot called Barracuda Point, where one can hang out at 80 or 90 feet on the point as the current streams past, offering up large schools of jack, barracuda, black snappers, rainbow runners, pairs of bigeye trevally, and usually a host of sharks, including not only the smaller blacktip reef sharks and whitetip sharks, but also the larger, and very muscular silvertip sharks. Very impressive!

One day, as we finished up a dive on Barracuda Point by poking around in the shallows on the far side of the point, we heard quite a bit of booming, similar to the explosions we had heard so long ago on Sipadan, but more muffled and almost continuous. Back on board, we asked our divemasters, Sam and Kellie, about it, and they said it was a nearby underwater volcano, which was in the process of creating a new island! We heard the same booming on the second dive we made at the same spot later that day. How extraordinary it was to hear the birth pangs of a new island!

Postscript: Los Angeles, February 1, 2009

It has been almost exactly three years since we first heard a humpback singing, and not surprisingly, I think of the experience often and with great fondness.

But what does surprise me is what triggers those memories this evening. Jon and I are attending an organ recital by Kevin Bowyer at the Walt Disney Concert Hall in Los Angeles. Halfway through, I realize that this concert is the only land-based experience I can think of that even begins to approach what it's like to swim with humpbacks.

Visually, the architecture of the concert hall evokes the ocean. Its exterior rises skyward in enormous waves of stainless steel plating, while inside, the undulating curves of the Douglas fir walls and ceiling engulf us and summon up memories of restless heaving ocean swells. We sit near the back of the main seating area, with a vast open space between us and the huge wooden pipes of the organ.

One piece in particular, *Trivium*, by contemporary organ composer Arvo Pärt, is filled with a range of tones and sounds, exotic and sometimes even bizarre, that to me are reminiscent of the sounds produced by the humpbacks—otherworldly sounds that cannot be described in words. All of this is remarkably similar to what we experienced with the whales, but one thing is missing: the tactile, visceral feeling of the whale's songs. We not only floated in those sounds, we actually felt them vibrate on our skin and resonate in our guts.

The last selection of the evening is Bach's *Passacaglia and Fugue in C minor*. As the music rises and swells, I can sense the air and the walls resonating with it. It builds inexorably to a massive crescendo of sound, and I close my eyes. My skin feels the touch of the music, and my whole body resonates. I am transported once more to that magical moment in the Caribbean when I first floated in the song of the whale. At this moment, it's as though I were sitting in the belly of the beast as he sings. And in a rush of recognition, I hear a deep watery voice in my mind saying "Welcome back!"

Azul profundo, indeed.

CHAPTER 21

The Cozumel "Special Effects" Dive

Paul

Most scuba divers engage in what is known as recreational diving—diving to a maximum depth of 130 feet and not staying underwater long enough to require a decompression stop. Other divers take the sport to another level and become technical divers. They venture down to over 200 feet, make long dives requiring a decompression stop, and in some cases also breathe an exotic mixture of gasses, including helium or a higher percentage of oxygen, instead of ordinary air. I'm a recreational diver, but occasionally I like to push the limits and try something different. So when dive buddy Fulvio, known to friends as Fulvio of the Deep (FOTD), suggested we try something different, I was intrigued.

"What do you have in mind?" I asked.

"Oh, you'll love this dive. My friend Rosendo invented a dive he calls his Special Effects Dive. He's the only divemaster in Cozumel who does it."

"Really? What's so special about it?"

"It's a wall dive. But instead of dropping down over the edge of the wall and then going deeper along the wall, we get dropped far out in deep blue water, where you can't see anything around you. Then we descend to about 100 feet or deeper and navigate toward the wall.

Soon it just appears out of the blue. It looks spectacular. At the wall, we ascend to about 80 feet and continue the dive until it's time to go up."

"And the boat will meet us when we surface?

"Usually. But if not, I bring this huge safety sausage so he can find us."

Fulvio shows me a bright yellow tube that inflates up to 12 feet in length, much larger than the safety tubes (sausages) most divers carry, which inflate to about 4 feet. "I guess that's good to have with you."

"Yes, sometimes the currents can run strong and carry you pretty far, so we need to be prepared."

"Sure," I agree, thinking about the possibilities of Cozumel's famously unpredictable currents sweeping us away.

Because of those currents, most wall dives begin with a descent to 40 or 60 feet over a sandy bottom. Then you swim to the edge of the wall and descend to around 80 feet, sometimes a little deeper, keeping close to the wall, which is covered with corals and colorful sponges. As you swim or drift along with the current, various creatures peer out from tiny crevices or outcroppings. A crab or lobster here, a large-eyed squirrelfish there, a spotted moray eel watching you warily as you approach. It's all captivating and totally engrossing.

Ahead, and a little deeper, you may see a hawksbill turtle munching on a juicy sponge surrounded by a cluster of angelfish snapping up the floating sponge crumbs—a symbiotic relationship at its best. You descend to investigate. The tricky part of the dive is that there is no visual bottom for reference since the wall continues down for another 1,000 feet. Consequently you might not realize your depth unless you monitor your depth gauge. It's an unsettling moment when the depth gauge reads 130 feet on a planned 80-foot dive. So you ascend to your planned depth, but no faster than your bubbles are rising—a visual safety guide. *Thank you, bubbles.*

However, for all the beauty of the wall and its interesting inhabitants, it is difficult get a true perspective of the wall's dimensions. As land-lubbers would say, you are so close that you "can't see the forest for the trees." Rosendo's Special Effects Dive provides a different perspective.

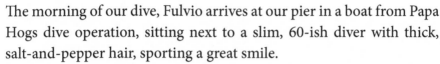

The morning of our dive, Fulvio arrives at our pier in a boat from Papa Hogs dive operation, sitting next to a slim, 60-ish diver with thick, salt-and-pepper hair, sporting a great smile.

"I am Rosendo," the diver announces in a friendly tone. We shake hands and start to set up our dive gear. Rosendo moves with the grace and alacrity of a man 20 years younger. There are several famous walls in Cozumel: Santa Rosa, San Francisco, Villa Blanca, and the one on which we will dive today, Cedral Wall, only a 15-minute boat ride from my pier. When we arrive at the dive site, our boat driver heads out toward deeper water. I have dived Cedral Wall as a typical wall dive in the past, but never from this far out. Rosendo gives us our dive briefing.

"We will descend quickly to between 100 feet to 120 feet. Follow me. When we reach the wall, ascend to 80 or 60 feet and finish the dive together."

The dive requires you to closely monitor your depth and air. A deeper dive means you use up air quicker so you have to surface sooner. You also must check your dive computer, which shows how long you can safely stay down at the present depth, and whether you must ascend to a shallower depth to avoid a decompression stop. Staying too deep for too long would require a decompression stop; not overly serious as long as you correctly perform the stop for the specified period of time to avoid decompression illness known as "the bends."

Before we jump in, I take a compass reading so I can navigate toward the wall in case we get separated. We roll backward off the boat and begin our descent. Fulvio drops like a rock. It takes me a little more time to clear or "equalize" my ears, so I descend more slowly but eventually catch up to him. I level off at 100 feet; Fulvio goes deeper, I estimate to 120 feet. Blue water diving is different from diving with a reference point. I am weightless, suspended in a blue void. The only sound is the bubbles exiting from my regulator with each breath. I spin around and see nothing, only blue, then I look down and see nothing, only more blue. I look up and see the brightness of the sun, and my bubbles rising toward the surface, shimmering and expanding as they rise. I see Fulvio below. His bubbles are passing me. They are strangely beautiful; no longer perfectly round as they rise, but flat on the bottom and rounded on top.

We remain together, so instead of navigating with my compass, I prefer to follow Rosendo as we begin our trek toward the wall. Underwater visibility is typical for Cozumel, over 100 feet. Around us, all I see is just clear blue water. I look around, expecting something large to swim out of the void, but all we see are schools of silvery jacks and blue creole wrasses. After several minutes, I strain to look ahead to where I think the wall should be. Soon, a mass begins to appear, then some details. Another minute and there it is: Cedral Wall, as I have never seen it before, a CinemaScope, widescreen portrait.

I look left and right, taking in the panoramic view. The wall is enormous! The ends disappear past our visibility. I look up and see that the wall extends upward to within 60 feet of the surface. Looking down, it disappears into the gloomy blue depths, past our 100+ foot visibility, more than 1,000 feet to the sea floor. I see Fulvio below me as we approach the wall.

Fulvio Approaches Cedral Wall   Cozumel, Mexico
Paul Mila Photo ©

Soon, detailed shapes appear, and we can discern leafy fan corals, round brain corals, bulky barrel sponges, and long tube sponges. This is, as Rosendo promised, truly a Special Effects Dive! We get a little closer and now our panoramic view includes muted colors. The fan corals appear purple, brain corals a gray-green, the barrel sponges look brown, and the tube sponges yellow. We are so deep, the blue water has absorbed the sunlight's red wavelength, but I know that some of the brown sponges would appear bright red if we shone a light on them up close.

Reaching the wall at 100 feet deep, I still have half a tank of air, but my computer informs me I need to ascend to a shallower depth. If I remain 5 more minutes at 100 feet, I will have to make a decompression stop before surfacing. Slowly following my bubbles up to 70 feet, my computer recalculates that I now have 20 minutes of safe dive time remaining. Soon, we see the usual creatures that make the reef home: a wide variety of fish, including French, queen and gray angelfish, grouper, filefish, and silvery mutton snappers. Spiny lobsters wave their whip-like antennae as we cruise past. I glance up and see a hawksbill turtle diving after a surface breath. I raise my SeaLife camera and take the shot just before he flies over my head.

Diving Hawksbill, Cedral Wall   Cozumel, Mexico
Paul Mila Photo ©

We continue exploring the reef, but we've been underwater almost an hour now. All of us are getting low on air, so we assemble at 15 feet for a 3-minute safety stop. Popping up to the surface moments later, we see our dive boat off in the distance. We wave but our boat driver doesn't see us. Fulvio uses the air in his tank to inflate his giant sausage. The driver spots us and we float around, laugh and talk about our spectacular dive as he makes his way over to retrieve us. Five minutes later, we are all back on board. On the ride back to the pier, I thank Rosendo and Fulvio for treating me to a unique view of a natural underwater wonder that few divers ever experience. Rosendo's Special Effects Dive turned out to be very special.

A sad footnote to this story. I learned that Cozumel dive legend Rosendo Espejel passed away about a year after he took me on two of his Special Effects Dives. Rosendo was a true gentleman, and the Cozumel dive community misses him.

CHAPTER 22

A DAY IN THE LIFE

Judy

From the very first moment I saw and heard humpback whales, I wished fervently that I had a Babel fish to stick in my ear so I could understand those haunting sounds flowing around and through me in the vast blue liquid of the ocean. The Babel fish was an invention of Douglas Adams in his science fiction series, *The Hitchhikers Guide to the Galaxy*. This tiny yellow fish is capable of translating any language to any other language. If you stick one of them in your ear, you can immediately understand what any alien is saying. *Even*, I thought, *humpback whales.*

While all whales make sounds, only the humpbacks are recognized as creating songs. The whales also use sounds (as distinct from the community songs) as a means of communicating among themselves. If you have listened to any recordings of humpback sounds, the first thing you might notice is the extraordinary range of sounds they make. It is extremely difficult to represent these sounds phonetically because they differ so radically from human speech. Here is a partial listing of how I describe some of these sounds:

❖ Chirp

❖ Weeoooo

- ❖ Trill
- ❖ Creaking-door-hinge
- ❖ Yawning-gates-of-hell
- ❖ Moo
- ❖ Waaooo
- ❖ Acid-indigestion
- ❖ Jungle-beast-roar
- ❖ Elephant-trumpet
- ❖ Flup-flup-flup
- ❖ Rhino-mutter
- ❖ Earthquake-rumble
- ❖ Garuf-bip
- ❖ Hysterical-chihuahua-yip
- ❖ Strained-rigging-on-a-ship-at-midnight

In addition, these "basic sound units" may occur at various pitch levels and with either a rising or falling intonation. Some of the low-pitched sounds, by their nature, are more felt than heard. For example, the low-pitched acid-indigestion sound causes vibration in the chest of the observer, whereas yawning-gates-of-hell tends to vibrate in the sinuses. A full-up earthquake-rumble rattles every bone in your body from your cranial bones all the way down to the phalanges of your little toes.

But what do these sounds *mean*? Join me as I pop an imaginary Babel fish in my ear and jump into the water to experience my admittedly fanciful take on a day in the life of the humpbacks of the southern Pacific Ocean.

Note: Although the whale names and dialogues I've created here are totally fictitious, I have actually observed the behaviors described during our trip to Tonga. What I've tried to capture in these tales is my sense of the spirit and intent of these fascinating mammals. In other words, I'm anthropomorphizing. Deliberately. And with mischief aforethought.

It is 6:15 a.m. on a lovely August morning in the waters of the Ha'apai Island Group of the Kingdom of Tonga just west of Uonukuhihifo Island and Uonukuhahaki Island. (I will refer to them as U-U.) The two islands stretch north to south like a pair of long, skinny, and somewhat lumpy sausages, conjoined by a narrow sand bridge. Our friendly leviathans are still sleeping—well, half-sleeping is more accurate. Because they are air-breathing mammals and must control their breathing consciously, only half of their brain sleeps at any moment, while the other half assumes night watch, controlling their slow ascend-breathe-descend movements.

In the shallow waters close to the islands, a mother rises and sinks in her half-sleep on about a 20-minute cycle, while her baby's breathing cycle is much shorter, about 10 minutes long. Mama's name is trill/trill/rhino-mutter\flup-flup-flup/, which my Babel fish translates as Star-Gazer. Her 3-month-old daughter's name is waaooo/weeooo\garuff-bip/hysterical-chihuahua-yip\, which translates as Rain-Gulper. Star-Gazer has been observed doing frequent spyhops, rising vertically in the water until her rostrum and eyes are out of the water, and Rain-Gulper is inordinately fond of swimming around on the surface with her mouth open during rainstorms, sticking her tongue out to catch and taste the strange saltless water.

As the sun rises over U-U, Baby Rain-Gulper slides under Mama Star-Gazer to collect her breakfast. Star-Gazer ejects her thick rich milk into the water in huge globules, which Rain-Gulper eagerly consumes. She is accompanied by a flurry of small fish that swoop in to feed on the floating leftovers.

Baby mutters, "Mmm, mmm, yummy!"

After breakfast, the two swim leisurely southward along the shore until they reach a favorite playground area.

Star-Gazer speaks to her baby. "Okay, dear one, this morning I will teach you how to do tail slaps."

Mom then proceeds to lift her flukes up out of the water and flexes her powerful muscles to bring her flukes crashing down flat on the surface with a satisfying THOMP that raises a maelstrom of foaming white water.

Rain-Gulper tries valiantly to imitate her mother, struggling to control her body with her floppy diminutive pectoral fins (which, to be more accurate, should be called arms), and after several attempts, manages to produce a petite but decent thomp of her own. Having gotten the hang of the trick, the two proceed to slap their tails in unison several times, just for fun, before they turn and lope westward into deeper waters. As they move, Rain-Gulper stays close to her mother, instinctively engaging in traditional baby-whale lolly-gagging. She touches Mom with her pecs, hugs close under her belly, swims up over her back, and rolls lazily across her huge rostrum. Star-Gazer, for her part, swims slowly, nuzzling her baby gently to ensure that she surfaces frequently to fill her small lungs with air.

First Tail Slap Lesson for Rain-Gulper   Tonga, South Pacific
Photo Courtesy of Jon Fellows ©

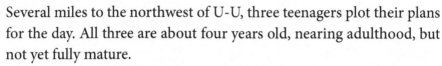

Several miles to the northwest of U-U, three teenagers plot their plans for the day. All three are about four years old, nearing adulthood, but not yet fully mature.

Swims-With-Sharks says to his best friend, "Hey, Frank-the-Crooner. Let's go play with the new tub toys!" (According to my Babel fish, tub toy is a somewhat loose translation of a phrase that actually refers to human-built boats. Obviously, whales don't have bathtubs, but they do enjoy playing with toys.)

Frank-the-Crooner responds, "Great idea, Swims-With-Sharks! I saw a really big one earlier this morning, heading west-southwest from Star-Gazer's lagoon."

Leaps-for-Joy, their teenage gal-pal chimes in with, "Hey, that sounds like fun. I'll show you the new game I invented with them!"

The three friends immediately turn and lope off at an easy six mph toward their objective. As they near the boat, Swims-with-Sharks spy-hops to get a better look at the curious object and observes that there are a dozen or more humans along the railing, pointing at him and his two friends, and shouting at each other excitedly.

"Cool!" he says and continues to move closer with his friends.

When they get within about two whale's lengths of the boat, Leaps-for-Joy says, "Okay, guys, watch this!" She then dives low and uses her powerful, muscular tail to propel herself vertically up and out of the water, arching parallel to the boat, and slamming back into the water on her side with a resounding WHOMP accompanied by a huge spray of foaming white water.

Her two friends watch in delight as the funny little humans on the boat screech and shout and clap. Not to be outdone, Frank-the-Crooner swims directly toward the side of the boat and at the very last moment, tucks his head and humps his back as he smoothly lifts his great flukes out of the water and dives directly under the boat. He hovers at 50 feet for a few minutes and then surfaces on the opposite side of the boat, emitting a satisfying BAWOOSH of spray from his

Leaps-For-Joy Does a Breach   Tonga, South Pacific
Photo Sequence Courtesy of Jon Fellows ©

blowhole. He looks back to watch all the humans rush from one side to the other, shouting and jumping and waving their undersized pectoral fins wildly.

Swims-with-Sharks and Leaps-for-Joy rejoin Frank-the-Crooner and move away from the boat, but then Swims-with-Sharks notices that the boat has turned and is following them.

"Hey," he says, "let's stick around for a while. We can have some more fun with these humans."

The Babel fish informs me that the whale word it has translated as "human" would translate more accurately as something like scrawny-spastic-crustacean, but being sensitive to my feelings, it has opted for a more politically correct word.

For an hour or so, the trio stays with the boat, spyhopping and breaching, positioning themselves on opposite sides of the boat so they can watch the humans run repeatedly from rail to rail. Swims-with-Sharks shows off by floating along on his side, lifting one of his powerful 10-foot-long pecs out of the water and slapping the surface forcefully over and over again. Occasionally, Leaps-for-Joy and Frank-the-Crooner execute tandem flukes-up dives, taking pride in the smoothness and skill with which they synchronize their movements. And best of all, the three friends discover that if they position themselves just so, they can entice the boat to move around and around in an effort to follow their antics, making it spin like a slow-motion top as it bobs on the swells. As the humans on the boat shout and chatter and cheer among themselves, so, too, the whales talk among themselves and emit torrents of whale chuckles, punctuated now and then with a gargantuan whale guffaw.

After a while, our three friends grow bored with their rather clumsy tub toy and set off to the northwest in search of new adventures, easily outpacing the far slower human boat. For a few minutes, the boat sits alone, befuddled and forlorn, but then it, too, takes off to find new adventures.

Heading north-northeast, it chances upon another trio of humpbacks, this time adults. Two males, Handsome-Pecs and Wave-Basher, are courting a female, Shapely-Flukes.

Handsome-Pecs tries his best pickup line. "Hey, baby, I'd sure like to cruise with *you!*"

Shapely-Flukes refuses to dignify this line with a reply. Instead, she chooses to lope along and ignore this rather-too-obvious male. Handsome-Pecs escalates with a series of pec slaps, his specialty, as he cruises beside Shapely-Flukes. Meanwhile, Wave-Basher does his best power dive as he crosses directly in front of the other two, hoping to divert Shapely-Flukes's attention. She definitely notices him but isn't about to let on that she's intrigued. At the bottom of his dive, Wave-Basher catches her eyeing him, which inspires him to shoot for the surface, executing three magnificent breaches in a row.

Well, of course, this prompts Handsome-Pecs to bellow, "Hey buddy. Go chase a school of sardines. This babe is mine!"

Wave-Basher responds, "Au contraire, mon ami, zees 'babe' as you say, is an independent female, free to choose whom she weeshes as her lovair."

Turns out, Wave-Basher is a foreigner from a population that frequents Tahitian waters, and Shapely-Flukes finds the foreigner and his accent charming. She hums her most fetching smile and edges in his direction, circling seductively. Wave-Basher hangs vertically, tail almost touching the surface, and sings the local group's courting song with just the slightest Tahitian-French accent.

In response, Handsome-Pecs charges toward Wave-Basher, circling him with a menacing bubble curtain formed by forcing air through his blowhole. Well, that's just more provocation than Wave-Basher is willing to tolerate, and his response is quick and definitive. He curves up to the surface for a quick breath of air, then power dives directly toward Handsome-Pecs, broadsides him with an emphatic head butt, and pushes him away from Shapely-Flukes.

She offers an appreciative vocal approval, which translates roughly as, "Now that's my kind of male!" She swims toward Wave-Basher, swishing her flukes seductively and offering her vulnerable ventral side to him.

Wave-Basher moves toward her, singing fervently. "Come, my leetle damsel feesh, let us make magnifique musique togethair."

Meanwhile, Handsome-Pecs swims off into the blue, muttering, "Well, she wasn't all that great, anyhow. I'll go find myself a hotter dame."

As the day progresses, various small groups of whales roam throughout their huge watery territory, and the boat cruises slowly, following and watching.

About midafternoon, two of the more adventuresome and curious of the local teenagers, a male named Slow-Roller and a female named Sweet-Judy-Blue-Eyes (Seriously, that's how my Babel fish translates her name. I'm not making this up), decide to study the strange tub toy up close and personal. They cruise slowly over to the boat and begin to swim under and around it, spyhopping and lollygagging, generally just fluking around and having a whale of a time.

Watch them here:
http://tinyurl.com/flukes-up-duet

For the humans, this is extreme provocation, and they race along the deck, shouting and scrambling and stumbling all over each other in their haste to pile into their two tiny inflatable dinghies. Slow-Roller and Sweet-Judy-Blue-Eyes are pleased that they have enticed the humans to come and play with them. They swim past and circle the miniscule dinghies, as the humans slither headfirst like sea lions into the water and swim with the whales.

Well, Sweet-Judy-Blue-Eyes and Slow-Roller have never seen anything funnier in their lives! These pint-sized humans splash and bob in the water, all herky-jerky, and are obviously way too slow to keep up with them. But they are basically kindhearted whales, not to mention curious, so they slow down and circle around, repeatedly passing close to the humans.

Sweet-Judy-Blue-Eyes gets a close-up look at one of the humans and says to her friend, "Hey, Slow-Roller. Look at these humans. They actually have two teeny eyes back inside their one big eye. Isn't that bizarre?"

Slow-Roller responds, "Yeah, I noticed that, too. And they actually seem to be looking at us, like maybe they really are intelligent beings. I've never really believed that old whale's tale until now."

Then Sweet-Judy-Blue-Eyes experiences something totally freaky. One of the humans swims alongside her, looking directly in her eyes. Wow! It moves its skinny-mini pecs exactly the same way she's moving her pecs! Just to be sure she's not imagining things, Sweet-Judy-Blue-Eyes moves her pecs down, then does a small circular motion. Yep! The human does the same thing. Amazing!

"Hey, Slow-Roller. This one is actually imitating my movements!"

"Far out!" he replies, and then he sends out a call to the other whales in the vicinity. "Hey folks, come over here and see this. These humans are really something!"

From far and near, the whales gather, as captured in this brief video: http://tinyurl.com/three-humpbacks

Three come in from the northwest, two from the east, two others from somewhere to the south. They're all a bit more reticent than these two adventuresome teenagers, so they hang out about 50 feet down, milling around and gawking as the youngsters continue to play with their newfound human friends. The humans are mere midges, awkward and certainly very funny-looking, but the older whales in the congregation know about the old days, when humans hunted and killed their ancestors. Their hearts, which are as big as their voices, fill with new hope for the future.

Far too soon, the humans tire, clamber back into their dinghies, and return to their floating tub toy. The whales disperse and spend a few more hours roaming their great ocean homeland before once more settling down for their nightly half-sleep.

As they cruise and snooze, they think and dream of the strange little beings who entered their world today and touched their hearts.

CHAPTER 23

SHARK TALES

Paul

Most divers who have encountered sharks find them more fascinating than dangerous. The only predictable aspect of shark encounters is that they are unpredictable and can take many unusual twists and turns. Here are three situations in Cozumel, Antigua, and Montauk, Long Island.

Stubby the Nurse Shark

The sharks many divers frequently encounter during their Caribbean and Florida underwater adventures are nurse sharks. They can grow large, up to 14 feet, but most commonly are seen in the 6- to 10-foot range. With a broad body, almost flat on the bottom, and a long caudal (tail) fin, you can see how closely sharks are related to rays. They tend to rest during the day and are frequently found sleeping under coral outcroppings or just inside the mouth of a cave. Nurse sharks have docile natures compared to other shark species and tolerate close encounters with humans, up to a point. If divers move within several feet or try to touch a fin, the shark will move off. Some divers mistake nurse sharks' mild behavior for tameness. Big mistake! These are still wild animals with shark DNA. Accidents (bitten divers) happen when a bold (i.e. stupid) diver pulls a fin or pets the shark like a puppy. Their teeth are small and designed for crushing their typical prey—shellfish. Add to that a suction-type feeding behavior and the unfortunate diver who tries to cuddle a nurse shark may return home with a crushed hand, forearm, or worse.

Diving in Cozumel with my dive instructor Alison one afternoon, we encountered a small nurse shark about four-feet long, with an unusually small front dorsal fin. (Nurse sharks have a second dorsal fin back toward the tail.) Many adult sharks have missing or truncated fins due to aggressive mating behavior or due to fights to establish pecking order during feeding. Alison had seen this particular shark before and told me she thought it had been born with a deformed nub of its dorsal fin. She named him Stubby. On repeated encounters over the years, I watched Stubby grow from a four-foot youngster into a stout, eight-foot adult.

Stubby Exiting the Cave with a Remora Beard   Cozumel, Mexico
Paul Mila Photo ©

Diving Yucab Reef one morning, we prepared to ascend when Alison spotted Stubby below us, hunting along the coral. We descended and watched him corner his prey inside a small cave. Our group of four divers formed a semicircle at the cave opening. We watched Stubby thrash his long tail and force himself into the narrow opening to kill whatever he had trapped, probably a lobster. Half of his body protruded from the cave, shaking and thrashing as he made his kill. Seeing the violence of the attack, I was happy to be positioned at his rear rather than the business end. After a couple of minutes, the battle was over, and he lay still. Then his body shuddered, probably as he swallowed breakfast. When Stubby wiggled backward out of the cave sporting a "remora-fish beard," he was startled to see a bunch of bubble blowers around him.

Stubby turned quickly, and I shot another photo (below) as he swam away, right between my legs. I was glad his dorsal fin was "stubby"!

Stubby Passing Between My Legs   Cozumel, Mexico
Paul Mila Photo ©

A couple of years after my last Stubby encounter, Alison told me she had spotted Stubby trailing a fishing leader from his lower jaw. Alison never saw him again after that. Perhaps as an adult, Stubby had expanded his hunting range out of Cozumel's protected park and was taken by a fisherman. Or Stubby might have been captured by an illegal poacher within the park. I recently contacted Alison for background on this story.

She hopes Stubby migrated north and is happily swimming somewhere else. But she said, "I do not know why once reaching full adulthood he would begin to gradually move northward. There is a lot that I don't understand about nurse shark behavior; I just observe. The only thing for certain is that I really, really miss Stubby."

The most likely scenario, unfortunately, was that Stubby's fate has been the fate of too many other sharks—overfishing. In a mere 30 years, humans have reduced the worldwide shark population by 90%. As the demand in Asia for shark-fin soup and other shark by-products increases, the pressure on their dwindling population intensifies.

Bowling for Divers

Carol and I took a summer trip to the Caribbean island of Antigua with our friends, Marilyn and Michael Holland. Diving is included at the Sandals Resort where we stayed. Carol is the snorkeler of the group, but the three of us packed in as much diving as we could.

The dive site this particular day was called Billy's Grotto. Halfway through the dive, at about 60 feet, I spotted a long caudal fin and rear half of a fish protruding from a coral outcropping or shallow cave below us. From the size and shape of the fin, I knew it belonged to a very large nurse shark.

A Telltale Tail   Antigua
Paul Mila Photo ©

Common sense might have dictated to keep going. But we three adventurous souls decided to investigate what promised to be a large shark attached to this tail fin. We descended and gathered at the cave opening, expecting to see a single shark. But we were surprised to see not one but several large, husky sharks. Marilyn counted five, I saw three. Two faced us, resting on top of the shark whose tail fin we had spotted. They appeared to be sleeping. The thing about "sleeping" sharks is that because sharks do not have eyelids, you can't be sure they are really asleep.

Marilyn thought they were about to mate. Sharks are known to become extremely annoyed and agitated when their mating behavior is disturbed—just like humans. So Marilyn decided to quietly withdraw.

I recalled seeing videos of nurse sharks mating. It usually happens out in the open, where the males have room to maneuver the females into position by biting on their fins. But then again, I'm not a nurse shark sexpert.

Nurse Sharks Inside the Cave   Antigua
Paul Mila Photo ©

I wanted to get a good photo, but since the effective flash range underwater is only four or five feet, I had to venture farther into the cave and get closer for a good shot. Swimming deeper into a small cave 60 feet underwater inhabited by several large sharks, that might be either asleep or possibly planning a romantic encounter, might seem either brave or stupid, depending on your point of view. But I felt lucky and snapped off a couple of flash shots with my camera. The sharks stirred. Were they really asleep or watching me, hoping I would come closer and become an easy meal? I could not tell from their lidless shark eyes, but since they got more restless, the best option was to back out and rejoin Marilyn and Michael outside the cave.

Michael had already ascended over the top of the cave to see if there was a rear opening to the formation. Marilyn and I also ascended a few feet over the top of the cave entrance and looked down. Suddenly, one shark bolted out of the cave like a missile, in a cloud of sand. It happened so fast, I couldn't raise my camera quickly enough to take a shot. Seconds later, another shark exploded from the cave, followed by the third. Michael looked back, concerned that he could not see Marilyn and me through the spreading sandy cloud. He thought the sharks had rammed us in their panicked exit from the cave, but we all joined up safely several seconds later.

Nurse sharks are usually slow swimmers. Divers frequently observe them languidly swishing their long tails side to side as they patrol the sea floor searching for crustaceans. The three of us had never seen them swim so rapidly, using short, quick thrusts of their powerful caudal fins to propel themselves as if shot from a cannon. Later, we realized that had we remained in front of the cave opening, these sharks would have slammed into us like bowling balls, scattering us like bowling pins.

Caged

August on Long Island is beach weather, featuring balmy breezes and warm water. I had no Caribbean dive adventures planned, so I wandered into Scuba Network to inquire about a caged shark dive in Montauk aboard Captain Chuck Wade's *Sea Turtle*.

I had heard about these east-end shark encounters for a couple of years, and it seemed like an interesting thing to do, something different. Martha was busy in the store, but never too busy to chat about diving.

"So Martha, tell me about shark diving on the *Sea Turtle*."

"Oh it's amazing! I did it, and we saw lots of sharks."

"And you're in a cage, right?" I'm used to being in the water with Caribbean reef sharks and nurse sharks. Makos and blues are something else. These are pelagic species, deep-water, ocean-crossing sharks, more aggressive and more opportunistic than their Caribbean cousins when it comes to food. *Hey, not sure what this is, but let's sample a bite and see if it tastes good.* While it's not out of the question to swim with these sharks outside of a cage, it is a bit more risky. I decided a cage was the safe way to go. Maybe I really am Chicken of the Sea?

"Yes, you are in a cage. Very safe." Martha laughs. "My feet are so tiny I had to keep them away from the bottom of the cage because the sharks pushed against the bars for a nibble. Keeping my feet up, it looked like I was riding a bicycle. It was great fun!"

"Hmmm, I see." Now a shark-tooth pedicure has never been on my bucket list, but I figured, *What the heck. My feet are bigger than Martha's, I should be okay.*

"All right, Martha, sign me up."

Carol and I decided to combine a short Montauk vacation with my shark dive, since we always enjoy visiting the seafood restaurant, Gosman's Dock. I asked Carol if she was interested in joining me inside the cage, since you are not required to be a certified diver. The cage just hangs several feet below the surface and air tanks and regulators are attached to the sides. You just insert the mouthpiece and breathe. If you want to get back on the boat, simply ask the sharks to unlatch the door on top of the cage and let you out. No problem.

For some reason, Carol was not interested. She kept mentioning something about all these "what ifs." The night before we left for Montauk, about a two-hour drive from Carle Place, I heard her rustling through papers, mumbling something about life insurance policies.

We departed Carle Place before sunrise and arrived about 6:00 a.m. at the Montauk Marina where the *Sea Turtle* was docked. I met Captain Chuck Wade, his crew, and five other fearless adventurers, none of whom were divers. They were just out for the thrill of being in the water with sharks. All hands aboard, we pulled out of the harbor at 6:30 a.m., passing most of Montauk's famous fishing fleet still moored, and Gosman's Dock, where Carol and I had a date for a lobster dinner, unless one of those pesky "what ifs" happened. The morning was warm and sunny, almost no breeze, and the sea was flat. A nice day for a boat ride on the *Sea Turtle*.

We cruised for about an hour until we reached our destination, about 10 miles southeast off Montauk Point, where Captain Chuck expected to encounter sharks. Not much to do in the meantime, so I inspected the shark cage perched upside down on the stern. It looked very similar to the shark cage in which we all saw Richard Dreyfuss descend in *Jaws*. And we know how that misadventure turned out. But this cage seemed pretty sturdy. At least I couldn't bend the bars. Plus, the bottom was reinforced with a wire mesh covering, so I wouldn't be doing Martha's bicycle stroke to protect my tender toes.

Captain Chuck gave the non-divers a primer in how to breathe underwater through the regulators attached to two scuba tanks bolted to the side of the cage. Then he explained the protocol. When the sharks appeared, two of us would enter the cage through a hatch on top. The six of us would take turns, two at a time, watching the sharks circling our cage. After 15 or 20 minutes, we exit the cage, scramble onto the boat, and the next two get their chance to see the sharks. This would happen while the sharks circled the cage. I was about to ask if this was safe, and I vaguely recalled that this question was on Carol's "what if" list. Never mind.

We arrived at our destination, some GPS coordinates on Captain Chuck's map, and he chummed the water. He ladled the thick, gooey, bloody mess into the sea, hoping to attract sharks, eerily reminiscent of the famous scene from *Jaws*. Any minute, I expected a mouthful of sharp white daggers to explode from the deep, and I wondered if I would stumble backward into the cabin like Roy Scheider, babbling, "You're gonna need a bigger boat." I hoped not.

Almost two hours passed with no sharks. It turned out that weekend was the annual Montauk Shark Fishing Tournament, when rugged, macho outdoorsmen assert their manhood by hooking a passing shark with a rod and reel from the safety of their boats. Can you guess my editorial opinion on shark fishing?

Captain Chuck (Standing), Chumming for Sharks in the Morning Sun   Montauk, Long Island
Paul Mila Photo ©

Another hour passed with nary a triangular dorsal fin in sight. Well, at least the sea was calm, so no one got seasick. Yet every 10 minutes over the radio, we heard reports from the shark fishing boats. "Hey, we just caught another large blue shark."

Hmmm, I wondered, *was there any connection between their success and our lack of sharks to observe?* Sorry, another editorial opinion.

Another hour bobbing around the ocean and I was bored. Boredom is not a good condition for me. Being a certified control freak—my relatives, friends, and acquaintances will confirm this—I decided to take control of the situation. I recalled reading that some divers rub an empty plastic water bottle between their palms to attract sharks. The crackling noise is supposed to sound like a fish in distress and attract sharks. I don't recall if this theory was ever scientifically tested, but a control freak has to do something! So I drank the water in my plastic bottle and hung off the stern in the water up to my elbows, rubbing the empty bottle between my palms.

Captain Chuck watched me. He shook his head with a strange smile, like someone watching their crazy uncle dance with a lampshade on his head at a party. The others just ignored me.

"Do you really think that will work?" one person eventually asked.

I had no idea, but from above the surface I could hear the plastic bottle crackle underwater, which meant the sound was loud and could be heard down deep. I felt good. At least I was doing *something*.

After 10 minutes, one of the naysayers asked, "What happens if a shark comes? Will you see it?"

This was a good point. I hadn't thought about the possibility that a hungry, inquisitive shark might rocket out of the deep and attack the bottle in my hands. As I continued to operate my improvised, noisemaking, shark attractor, the mental image of me with no arms below my elbows seemed more and more unappealing. I thought, *Why should I be the only one going the extra mile trying to attract the sharks? I'm just a paying passenger. These bozos probably don't even appreciate my efforts. The heck with them; I quit!*

Five minutes later, someone pointed and yelled, "Shark!"

We turned toward the starboard side and saw the telltale triangular dorsal fin. It sliced the calm surface like a knife as it approached the *Sea Turtle*. The shark's sudden appearance could have been coincidental with my noise-making efforts, but I knew better. However, I resisted the temptation to say, *I told you so.* The shark circled the boat and Captain Chuck threw a few chunks of fish overboard to keep it interested. Next, he attached a whole fish, I think a mackerel, to a line without a hook to bring the shark closer to the boat.

"It's a young mako" he announced. "First mako we've seen all year."

It's the first mako I've ever seen in person, anywhere. The mako shark is reputed to be the fastest shark in the sea. Compared with other sharks I have encountered, I could see its streamlined form was built for speed. The body was sleek, like a torpedo, and the upper and lower lobes of its caudal fin were symmetrical, characteristics of fast, pelagic sharks. We saw its large black eyes, designed for hunting fast prey in the near-dark depths of the ocean. As Captain Chuck said, it was a juvenile. At about five feet in length, it would still grow, but already a very impressive fish.

"Okay," Captain Chuck announced. "Suit up and get into the cage."

Everyone else had a short, thin, 2-mil wetsuit. I knew that after standing relatively still inside a cage underwater in the Atlantic about 15 miles east of Montauk for about 20 minutes, my body would get cold. The water off the beach in Montauk was usually high 60s, low 70s at best and was probably cooler out here. I brought along a full-length, thick, 7-mil wetsuit. What I did not know is that the warm Gulf Stream spins off eddies as it brushes the East Coast before heading across the Atlantic toward Ireland. The *Sea Turtle* floated in one of these eddies, where the water almost reached 80 degrees. I quickly pulled on my thick wetsuit, and in the heat of the late-morning sun, I was soon boiling. I could not wait to jump into the water and cool off. I was glad Captain Chuck put me in group one.

Captain Chuck pushed the upside-down cage into the water, and with flotation devices on top, it righted itself. My selected lucky partner and I jumped in with our masks on and with our cameras and grabbed for the regulators hanging on opposite sides of the cage. In the warm water, I still felt overheated. So much for being the "expert" in the group. The shark kept busy chasing the baited line and did not approach the cage, which bobbed up and down, making it difficult to get good quality photos.

Still, it was exciting to snap some shots of this apex predator in its natural element. I watched it circle our cage as it made passes at the baitfish.

All too soon our 20 minutes were up. There was no alarm bell; we were strictly on the honor system. We wanted to give our fellow travelers their shot, so my partner and I exited the cage and scrambled

Chasing the Bait   Montauk, Long Island
Paul Mila Photo ©

A Close Pass   Montauk, Long Island
Paul Mila Photo ©

quickly onto the stern platform and then onto the boat. After almost an hour, the mako lost interest in us and swam off.

Hey buddy, keep away from the fishing fleet. I silently wished him well.

Everyone was ecstatic, and we exchanged impressions and observations. About 20 minutes later, a large blue shark approached, easily 12 feet long, a beautiful steely blue. We all suited up again. I was in group three this time. Compared to the mako, the blue shark was more slender and streamlined, with even larger black eyes and long pectoral fins, like wings. These are the long-haul experts of the ocean. Some blue sharks have been tagged and tracked migrating from the South Atlantic near Argentina to the North Atlantic near Europe.

Unfortunately, the blue shark departed when group two had been in the water for only a few minutes. My buddy and I didn't even get a chance to jump in.

We floated and chummed, chummed and floated, for another hour or two, with no results. Captain Chuck checked his watch. It was almost 4:00 p.m. He revved the engines and headed back to Montauk Harbor. I was disappointed we only got to see two sharks and only got into the water with one, but it was still a good day.

But as we continued to hear radio reports from the Rambo-Rodders, it was also a sad reminder that each year there are fewer and fewer sharks left patrolling our oceans.

I feel fortunate to have encountered sharks, the high-octane aspect of scuba diving, many times. But still on my bucket list is the apex of

Tattooed Captain Chuck and Me on the Way Home   Montauk, Long Island
Paul Mila Photo ©

shark encounters—cage diving with great whites. There are several places on Planet Ocean where divers can meet great whites through the relative safety of steel bars: South Africa, Australia, and Guadalupe, Mexico. Gaudalupe is closest, so that's my dive plan.

CHAPTER 24

A SHIVER OF SHARKS
AND OTHER OCEANIC COLLECTIVES

Judy

As scuba divers, Jon and I were eager to see *Finding Nemo* when it was released. The animation is remarkably realistic, recreating the colors and movements of tropical reefs and their inhabitants extremely well. The sharks, of course, are a hoot. The writers and animators have drawn on our deepest fears of these creatures to create razor-toothed nightmares of jaw-chomping menace—and then provided great comic relief by putting them in AA-style meetings where they must repeatedly remind themselves that "fish are friends, not food." As Paul has expressed so well, deep underneath our increasingly enlightened view of sharks, we are still fundamentally fascinated by our *fear* of them.

We were also delighted with how brilliantly the *Finding Nemo* animators capture the character and behavior of seagulls: noisy, bickering, quarrelsome, greedy, and avaricious. To call such a disreputable group of birds a flock doesn't even begin to convey their true nature. I think it would be much more accurate, not to mention colorful and descriptive, to call them a *squabble* of seagulls. Which brings me to the topic at hand: collectives.

The human mind has a strong propensity for grouping together things that are similar in some way and creating a distinct word for that grouping. In linguistics, these group words are called collective nouns. Some of these collective nouns (such as herd) are general purpose and can be used in a variety of situations. Not only can herd be used for cows, goats, and buffalo but also for inanimate things such as the herds of dust bunnies that continually plague my house. (Now that's one species I'd love to see become endangered.)

Some collectives have apparently been chosen because they imitate the sound or other sensory experience of the animals being described. Anyone who has ever seen (and heard) a large group of geese gathered together would most likely agree that gaggle of geese is much more descriptive (and entertaining) than the more mundane flock of geese.

Being a diver, I am particularly intrigued by the collective nouns used to describe oceanic creatures. Wikipedia provides a long list of such words, including the familiar:

❖ Swarm of eel

❖ Run of salmon

❖ Shoal of fish

❖ Bed of oysters

❖ Herd of manatees

❖ Pod of whales (or dolphins)

Some collectives are expressive of our human reaction to the animal in question, such as a shiver of sharks, which encompasses both our fascination and our fear. Similar collectives include:

❖ Fever of stingrays

❖ Glean of herrings

Other collectives seem to imitate the sounds (onomatopoetic) or behaviors of the animals:

❖ Scoop of pelicans

❖ Gulp of cormorants

❖ Fluther of jellyfish

Some collectives seem to have been chosen because they are alliterative (that is, the sounds of the words are repeated), such as:

❖ Battery of barracuda

❖ Consortium of crabs

❖ Grundle of groupers

That last one is a triple-header:

1. It is alliterative in that it repeats the initial "G" sound.

2. It includes a portmanteau word (grundle is a merge of grunt and trundle).

3. It is onomatopoetic in that it describes the "distinctly audible rumbling sound" produced by the fish when threatened (see http://tinyurl.com/goliath-grouper).

Having been engulfed in the middle of a large (hundreds) school of barracuda several times, watching enthralled as their glittering quicksilver bodies streamed sinuously past me, I would sacrifice the alliteration and choose to call them a *sleekness* of barracuda.

Other collectives seem to have no obvious explanation or rationale:

❖ Risk of lobsters

❖ Rout of snails

❖ Bale (or dule) of turtles

Well, I can perhaps see why a group of lobsters is a risk, given that there are many people who have a serious allergy to shellfish. But for those of us who do not have such allergies, something like a *feast* of lobsters would be more accurate.

But then we have the snails. I mean, seriously, a rout of snails? When have you ever seen a snail retreat at all, let alone in a hasty and disorderly fashion? Even if you consider the less common meanings of rout, there's no sense here. The *American Heritage Dictionary* lists the fourth meaning as, "a company, as of knights or wolves, that are in movement." Knights and wolves are one thing, but snails moving

as a company? Or take the fifth meaning. "A fashionable gathering."
Seriously? Fashionable snails?

Ah, but wait. We're talking about sea snails here, which would
include not only the bivalve (double-shelled) and the univalve (single-shelled) mollusks, but also their cousins the nudibranchs ("naked
gills") and the opisthobranchs ("gills behind" the heart). So now we're
talking some major fashion! From the yellow, black, and white pimply
surface of *Phyllidia ocellata*, to the sinuous (and vaguely obscene) purple, orange, and white cerata of *Cuthona sibogae*, or the stylishly sleek
black form of *Nembrotha kubaryana* with its teal green body stripes
and spots and orange-tipped rhinophores, or the pale lavender, cream,
and tan watercolor patterns of *Chromodoris coi*, these creatures definitely qualify (at least in my book, which is what you're reading right
now) as fashionable.

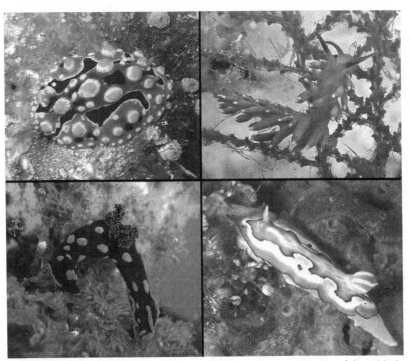

A Fashionable Gathering of Nudibranchs   Solomon Islands
Judith Hemenway Photos ©

Moving on down the list, I'm having real problems with a bale of turtles. By a rather lengthy stretch of the imagination, one could see a parallel between a single turtle and a "large package tightly bound with twine or wire" (such as a bale of hay), but how does one stretch such an image far enough to equate a group of turtles with a bale of hay? So is it that turtles are considered baleful? That means "portending evil, ominous." Oh come on now—turtles are evil? I'm aware that manta rays have been called devil fish as have the California gray whales, whose females are fiercely protective of their young and quite capable of attacking and smashing to pieces the whaling boats that once plagued them.

But if turtles have any imagery associated with them (other than the Surfer Dude characters in *Finding Nemo*, of course), it is that of creators. Eastern Woodland native societies, including both the Algonquian and the Iroquois, have creation stories in which it is Turtle who succeeds in diving to the bottom of the ocean to bring mud to the surface, creating the dry land that she then carried on her back. Thus, Turtle Island is the name given to the North American continent. And a Tongan legend centers on a turtle named Sangone, who was the mother of Hina of the Underworld. It was apparently Sangone who ensured the power of the Tu'i Tonga (religious ruler), as his power ended when Sangone's shell was sold in Fiji. So I would propose that a group of turtles be called a *creation* of turtles.

Of course, just as we have many pet names for our loved ones, we have a bountiful collection of collectives for our favorite ocean-going friends:

❖ Otters may be a romp, bevy, lodge, family, or raft

❖ Seals are a pod, rookery, bob, herd, or harem

❖ Sea lions may be called a pod, colony, crash, flock, harem, bob, herd, rookery, team, or hurdle

❖ Dolphins may be called a team, school, pod, herd, alliance (males), or party (females)

❖ Whales are a gam, pod, herd, or school

While I've rarely seen sea otters in the wild, I have observed them close up at both the Monterey Bay Aquarium and the San Diego SeaWorld facility. Although they lack the layer of blubber that insulates most other marine mammals, the otters have incredibly dense fur (about a million hairs per square inch) and a high metabolic rate to keep them warm. As a result, they are animated, active, and playful. To keep their metabolic fires burning, they must eat 25% or more of their body weight each day. Since their food consists largely of mollusks, the otters have learned to use rocks as tools. They float on their backs with their snail dinner on their tummies, and use their front paws to hold and smash the rock over and over again against the hapless snail until its shell cracks open. Given their frenetic playfulness and their delightfully inventive eating habits, calling a group of otters a romp seems perfectly fitting.

Groups of both seals (earless pinnipeds, the true seals) and sea lions (eared pinnipeds) are most commonly called herds, and their shore-based hauling out and breeding locations are called rookeries. The term harem is somewhat misleading and inaccurate, since only some species (like the elephant seals) actually form stable single-male multiple-female breeding groups. For other species (such as sea lions), the females are more independent and may move from one rookery to another. Given their propensity for poking their noses up out of the water to have a look around, the rarely used collective bob is an apt choice.

On one of our local California dive-boat weekends, we anchored at the sea lion rookery on Santa Barbara Island. I was teaching my 9-year-old niece how to snorkel, and we gradually worked our way in toward shore. Chelsea was captivated by a large group of pups on shore that were apparently being given swimming lessons by three adults. The adults would trumpet to the youngsters who would then dash awkwardly into the water, splashing and barking and honking. They would swim around in the surf briefly and then head back to shore. And then they would repeat the whole exercise again.

As we snorkeled closer, the pups turned their attention to us and came out almost to where we were. Imagine this scene: two human snorkelers tread water, their heads bobbing in the choppy waves as they stare intently at a large group of sea lion pups, whose heads are also bobbing in the choppy waves as they stare intently at the two snorkelers. The two snorkelers laugh and shout at each other excitedly, while the pups bark and honk and chatter among themselves with great animation. Given this experience, I suggest that a group of sea lion pups should be called a *bobble*. (And did you know that a baby spiny anteater is called a puggle? Sorry. I know that's totally irrelevant, but the word is so cute I had to put it in here.)

And then we have the dolphins and whales, which are probably the most beloved of all sea creatures. Mammals like us, they are social, intelligent, sleek, agile, and totally captivating. In groups, they are most commonly called pods, but sometimes herds or schools. Additionally, a group of male dolphins may be called an alliance and a group of females a party (hmmm, a bit of sexism, perhaps?). But to me, all of these terms miss the exceptional nature of these remarkable animals.

Dolphins are fast, powerful, and highly intelligent, as both the US Navy and SeaWorld have demonstrated. And anyone who has ever stood on the bow of a boat, slicing at 10 or 12 knots through sparkling, sunlit ocean swells, and watched a group of dolphins racing, leaping and frolicking in the whooshing bow waves, must surely agree with Herman Melville who wrote:

> "They are the lads that always live before the wind. They are accounted a lucky omen. If you yourself can withstand three cheers at beholding these vivacious fish, then heaven help ye; the spirit of godly gamesomeness is not in ye."

Godly gamesomeness, indeed! Thus, I propose that they be called an *exuberance* of dolphins.

And finally, of course, we have the whales or cetaceans. Both the toothed whales (*odontocetes*) and the baleen whales (*mysticetes*) are mammals whose land-based ancestors returned to the sea 50 million years ago. Their skeletons reveal vestigial rear legs, and their powerful front flippers or pectoral fins are actually modified arms with the same humerus, radius, ulna, wrist and hand bones as humans. They lack only our opposable thumb.

These enormous animals have fascinated us for as long as we have written records and probably for millennia before that. The constellation Cetus is named for the sea monster Ceto, slain by the Greek hero Perseus. The Old Testament book of Jonah says that Jonah was swallowed by a whale (or large fish), and of course, Melville's Captain Ahab pursued and was destroyed by Moby Dick, a huge white sperm whale.

At 100 feet long and close to 200 tons in weight, the blue whale is believed to be the largest animal that has ever existed (at least here on Earth).

I have been extraordinarily fortunate in my diving career to have had multiple close-up encounters with whales: gray whale mothers and babies in the birthing lagoons of Baja California; killer whales and a pilot whale at SeaWorld; Atlantic humpbacks at Silver Bank, their Caribbean nursery; and Pacific humpbacks in Tonga.

Of these many encounters, one of the most extraordinary experiences I have ever had was in Tonga. It was August 19, 2007, our 6th day aboard the Nai'a, plying the waters of Tonga's Ha'apai island group in search of humpbacks. We had already had many in-water encounters with these incredible mammals, and it seemed as though each day brought even more remarkable incidents.

We found a place where several small groups had converged and were willing to play with us. At one point as I was happily snorkeling with the whales on the surface, it occurred to me to look down. Shafts of sunlight sliced and danced through the infinite blue moving waters that buoyed me, but I could not see very deep because the entire ocean beneath me at about 50 feet down was filled with whales! There were 8 or 9 of them—impossible to get an exact count because they were in constant motion. These were all young adults and full adults, ranging in size from probably 20 to 35 feet in length. We really couldn't see the ocean for all the whales! There were about 20 of us snorkelers plus all the whales plus the two skiffs—a gargantuan free-for-all! Skipper Rob says he had never before seen that many whales at once, and he has been doing the trips to Tonga for 12 years.

Divemaster Richie and one of the other snorkelers saw a shark, which inspired us to get out of the water for a while, but the whales remained and we simply couldn't resist jumping (slithering as Rob says) back in. It was at that point that I got close to two whales and had extended eye contact with one of them. I approached the nearer whale to within about 10 feet and positioned myself so I could swim side by side with her. (I don't know whether it was a male or female, but I simply cannot bring myself to call such a creature an "it.") I saw her looking at me, so I put my arms down in a pecs-back position and held her gaze for a half minute or so. I slowly lifted and pointed my camera, took a shot (no flash), and then, just as slowly, the whale moved off.

Incredible! If you have never gazed into the eye of a whale, you have missed a truly profound experience. Dogs are intelligent, and will look at you, but they look at your surface—your facial expressions, body movements, etc. Even the orangutans and other great apes I have seen seem only to look *at* you. But when a whale looks at you, s/he is looking *into* you, eye to eye, probing for your essence. When you look at a whale, you cannot doubt that there is an intelligent being inside those eyes looking back at you. It is a truly magical experience. Based on this extraordinary encounter, I propose—no, I insist—that a group of whales be called a *magnificence* of whales.

You might ask, then, what would I call the entire collection of extraordinary experiences I have had in the 40+ years I've been diving? An *exhilaration*!

CHAPTER 25

THE FLYING EAGLE RAYS OF COZUMEL

Paul

Stingrays usually make the news for the wrong reasons. One of the most widely reported encounters involved the late Steve Irwin, the famous and fearless alligator hunter, who was fatally stabbed in the heart by a large bull ray several years ago. Then, weeks later, an 80-year-old grandfather was stabbed in the chest and heart with near-fatal results when a juvenile spotted eagle ray launched itself from the water landing in his boat. Have the creatures of the ocean declared war on mankind? The answer is a resounding "No!"

According to news accounts, Steve Irwin hovered over a large bull ray when a camera man positioned himself in front of the ray to get a shot. Normally, when a ray senses a predator, usually a shark approaching from above and behind, the ray bolts ahead for safety. If trapped, the ray will lash upward with its stinger, located at the base of its tail, inflicting a serious wound on the attacker. In this situation, the ray likely felt trapped by the camera man in front, lashed upward and struck Irwin in the chest.

The 80-year-old grandfather was simply in the wrong place at the wrong time. An eagle ray, probably spooked near the surface by passing boat traffic, accidentally leapt into the boat and landed in the man's

lap. Before the unfortunate boater could jump out of the way, the panicked ray lashed upward with stinger and caught him in the heart.

Over the last decade, the pendulum of human interaction with sea
creatures has swung from irrational terror, through the arc of respect,
and now rests at the extreme end of dangerous complacency. We have
become so comfortable that we forget we are dealing with wild animals who possess deadly self-defense mechanisms provided by mother
nature that enable them to survive another day.

There are 200 species of stingrays, ranging from small yellow stingrays, only one foot across, to giant manta rays, featuring 20-foot wing-
spans. Southern stingrays and eagle rays are two of the most common
rays encountered by divers in Caribbean waters. I've encountered both
species in the Cayman Islands, Roatan, Bonaire, and Cozumel.

Spotted Eagle Ray   Cozumel, Mexico
Paul Mila Photo ©

Diving in Cozumel, you expect to enjoy encounters with a wide
variety of sea life: moray eels (green, spotted, and golden), nurse
sharks, turtles (hawksbill, loggerhead, and green), huge lobsters, and
giant barracuda, just to name a few. But the favorite critters on my
wish list are always the spotted eagle rays. Watching a ray blot out the
sun as it soars overhead or glides gracefully beneath you during your

safety stop is a heart-stopping moment. Seeing even just one or two eagle rays during a dive trip is a treat.

Spotted eagle rays are beautiful creatures. As their name implies, their black dorsal area is covered with white spots. Their ventral area is uniformly white. They sport a long, thin, whip-like tail, five to ten feet long. Several venomous spines are located at the base of the tail. They are one of the larger rays, with a wingspan measuring up to 10 feet across. Their swimming technique differs from most other stingray species, which ripple their fins for propulsion. The eagle rays beat their wings, flapping them like aquatic eagles. Their snouts are almost pig-like, designed for digging through the sand to eat their favorite prey—crustaceans and mollusks.

Spotted Eagle Ray, Ventral View   Cozumel, Mexico
Paul Mila Photo ©

I had always wanted to dive Cozumel's Eagle Ray Alley ever since I had heard about the schooling eagle rays that gather at the northern end of the island during the winter months. No one knows where the rays migrate for the rest of the year, but they arrive in Cozumel in

November and hang around through March. I knew that my friend, Cozumel resident Fulvio, had made this dive many times.

I asked him about it and he said, "There might not be any other place in the world where you can get face-to-face with such a large squadron of them. I certainly have not heard of this from any other diver in my travels to many places. It's so unique and magical, really."

So on a March visit to Cozumel, Fulvio arranged a trip with Papa Hog's dive operation to visit the eagle rays. Early one morning, we left Papa Hog's dive shop, located next to the Villa Blanca Hotel, with four other divers. The day was sunny, not much wind, and the sea calm— perfect dive conditions. Passing the cruise ship pier, our 30-foot dive boat was dwarfed by the massive, 1,000-foot sweeping black hull of the 2,700 passenger Disney Ship, *Magic*. We waved "hi" to Mickey and kept on going.

About 10 minutes later, we arrived at the dive site. Eddie, our divemaster, gave us our dive briefing. He instructed us to descend quickly to 70 feet and then farther down to around 90 feet at the top edge of the wall.

It's a challenging dive, best attempted by advanced divers due to the strong currents. Fulvio had done this dive many times and was his usual bouncy self. I was more subdued; enthusiastic about doing a dive that I had wanted to experience for many years but apprehensive about the need to descend quickly because of the famous currents I had heard so much about. Eddie told us he might descend below us to 120 feet in case the rays remained deep and needed some encouragement to come up and play.

The currents at that location can be wicked, three to four knots, and can sweep careless divers off the wall. So we had to descend quickly, hang onto a convenient rock, and wait for the rays to show up. Otherwise, we might miss them, or in a worst case scenario, the *Cozumel Express* might sweep us toward Cancun, about 50 miles north.

We followed Eddie's instructions and descended quickly to the sandy bottom, perfect eagle ray hunting territory. Then we swam to the edge of the wall and descended another 20 or 30 feet, hunkered down, and waited. Here, the wall was covered by massive sponges, large coral formations, and protruding rocks. Visibility was the usual gin-clear 100-foot Cozumel vis. I looked behind me and saw that Fulvio had grabbed onto a large barrel sponge. He appeared relaxed, even though the current had stretched him out, hanging over the 1,000-foot abyss. His fins flapped like flags in the wind. I laughed through my regulator, grabbed a convenient rock with one hand, and held my camera with the other.

Suddenly, several rays appeared out of the deep blue, like apparitions "flying" along the edge of the wall. We watched them pass us, swimming effortlessly *into* the current.

Eagle Rays in Formation.   Cozumel, Mexico
Paul Mila Photo ©

A short YouTube video of the rays swimming in formation:
http://tinyurl.com/eaglerays-formation

I looked ahead and gulped, forgetting to breathe for a moment! Five more large eagle rays approached, like fighter jets flying a diamond formation. I estimated their wingspan was eight to ten feet across.

The YouTube video showing the rays as they approached:
http://tinyurl.com/eaglerays-approach

Divemaster Eddie had told us to remain calm and not approach or chase the shy animals because we would spook them. Our patience was rewarded as the rays soon became curious. After a flyby, they looped around and treated us to some close encounters. The action was so fast and intense that I had trouble deciding whether to shoot video or still photos. Luckily, my SeaLife 1400 camera toggled quickly between still and video modes, so I didn't miss any shots.

The culmination of the encounter occurred when one large eagle ray I had been watching turned and approached me. Typically, these timid animals will veer away before coming close, but this ray kept coming. I raised my camera and started shooting as it rapidly closed the distance between us, 60 feet, 40 feet, 20 feet. I watched in awe as it pumped its muscular body, beating its massive 10-foot wings. My heart stopped as it "flew" only a couple of feet over my head, so close that I could see its gills pumping water. I expected to feel some back-wash as it passed, but the ray was so streamlined I felt nothing. *Wow!* It was the photo-op of a lifetime. I was thrilled to have captured the all-too-brief moment on video!

The YouTube video showing the ray flying over my head:
http://tinyurl.com/eagleray-flyover

All too soon the rays departed, disappearing into the deep blue of the abyss. Fulvio swam up to me and we exchanged underwater hi-fives over our successful trip. Eddie signaled it was time to surface. Because of the deep depth and exertion fighting the strong current, this was a relatively short dive, 35 to 40 minutes. We ascended for our 15-foot safety stop, drifted together, and 3 minutes later surfaced. Our dive boat captain had followed our bubbles, so our water taxi was right there to meet us as we bobbed in the waves. We climbed aboard, exhilarated by our experience. Our conversations were animated as we compared notes over who had the closest encounter or who got the best photos. Our boat headed back to shore, carrying six happy divers, whooping and hollering about our exciting visit with the eagle rays. Back on dry land, I had time to reflect on our dive. Sometimes a "special, must-do dive" turns out to be a ho-hummer, but this one exceeded my expectations.

If you are ever diving in Cozumel during the winter months, add Eagle Ray Alley to your list of dive requests.

CHAPTER 26

SIMPLY SPLENDID

Judy

While diving Columbia Shallows off the coast of Cozumel, Divemaster Alison masterfully orchestrated and guided our group of eight divers, including the newly certified family of four, throughout the dive. She's the same Alison who taught Paul and his daughter to dive. (It's relationships like these that make strangers feel like family the moment you meet them.)

As individual divers ran low on air, she ensured that each of them made their safety stops and were back on the surface being picked up by the boat before turning her attention back to the rest of us. Since we were drift diving in fairly strong current with rougher-than-normal surface chop, we knew we all needed to stay together. Alison proved to be expert at riding herd on us. It was clear that she not only loved diving, but also thoroughly enjoyed being "den mother" to her charges.

We were nearing the end of our second dive when Alison motioned me over to a rugged outcropping of reef. She pointed out a five-foot long nurse shark that lazed on the sand at the base of the reef. Ah, that brought back fond memories of my first visit to Cozumel, 39 years previously! Jon and I were on our honeymoon and that was our first dive trip to tropical waters. It was also the first time I had ever seen a live shark in the water, and I didn't know at the time that nurse sharks are quite harmless. All I knew was that it was definitely a shark, which inspired me to discover that I could actually backpedal with my jet fins. I enjoyed reminiscing about that first encounter as I gave this particular specimen an appreciative inspection.

My attitude toward sharks has certainly changed over the years. They are truly beautiful and graceful creatures. The skin of a nurse shark is a soft brown color, and its shape is one I find particularly pleasing. A rounded nose merges smoothly with its sleek bullet-shaped body, and its two dorsal fins are placed far back on its body, leading gently to its long, gracefully curved scythe-like tail.

I nodded appreciatively to Alison who then directed my gaze to a hollow spot under a nearby small overhanging ledge. The beam of her light revealed a marvelously strange creature. All I could see was its head, the rest of its body being tucked securely back in its hidey-hole under the ledge. But what a head! Its face was broad, flat, and rounded, its wide-spaced eyes stared up at me with what I imagined to be a rather impertinent attitude. A somewhat irregular pattern of dark and light gray-lavender stripes splashed across its face from cheek to cheek. A finer variant of the same striped color scheme decorated its lips and radiated down and out from where a nose might be, if it had had one. The margin of its lower jaw, again from cheek to cheek, sported a couple dozen fat, fleshy lavender "whiskers" of varying sizes. Near one side of its head, a bright yellow patch indicated a half-hidden pectoral fin.

I had never seen anything like it before! With that thought, my attention shifted instantly to the empty camera housing I carried. Having suffered through several flooded camera incidents early in our diving careers, we have long been in the habit of pressure-testing the housing first, before we committed the actual camera to the perils of the deep. *Ah well, perhaps there will be other opportunities.* And then, of course, I remembered Finagle's Law: the Universe tends toward a maximum of perversity.

Paul's Photo Captures Almost Exactly What I Saw   Cozumel, Mexico
Paul Mila Photo ©

After the dive, I asked Alison what that strange fringy-faced fish was, and she said it was a splendid toadfish (*Sanopus splendidus*), which is found only in Cozumel. Fabulous! I had not seen one on that first trip so long ago, nor did I know such a creature existed. Toadfish are similar to our California native sculpins in that both sculpins and toadfish are bottom-dwellers that like to ambush their prey. However, sculpins are extremely well-camouflaged, while in contrast, this toadfish is decorated more like a circus clown with its bold lavender stripes and bright yellow fins.

I made sure I had my camera with me on every dive after that, but of course, Finagle looked over my shoulder the whole time, and I got to the point where I imagined I could hear his slightly deranged chuckle as part of the constant background water noise on every dive. (I read later in Wikipedia that male toadfish "sing" to attract females, so perhaps what I heard was the mating song of a confused toadfish.)

In spite of my disappointment at not getting a photo, we definitely enjoyed the diving and our stay on Cozumel. It was in some ways strange to return here after almost four decades—so much was familiar, and yet so much had changed.

In 1974, Cozumel had been a sleepy backwater of an island, with a total population of less than 12,000. Most lived in the little town of San Miguel. At the time, San Miguel had one wharf, which housed a dozen small fishing boats. We stayed at Cabañas del Caribe, one of a handful of small hotels located on the beach north of town. El Presidente, the one hotel south of town, was about 3 miles down. The rest of the shoreline on the west and all of the eastern (windward) shore was uninhabited.

Two of the small local fishing boats served as our dive boats; each could carry a maximum of eight divers. Every morning the boats picked us up at the small pier at our hotel and ran south to the extensive reef complex that paralleled the west coast of the island for about 12 miles south of San Miguel. Depending on location and water conditions, our dives were either anchored or drift dives. The anchored dives gave us a chance to explore a particular reef area in detail, nose around the corals, observe the fish (parrotfish, several varieties of angelfish, tangs, groupers, trunkfish, butterflies, wrasses, and many more), marvel over the huge variety of sponges—whatever suited our fancy. The drift dives gave us a free and effortless tour along the length of the reef structure, as though we rode a slow train and watched the scenery move past. In either case, the water was as warm as a bath and crystal clear. From the bottom at 80 or 100 feet, we could easily see the bottom of our boat—an astounding thing for us California divers who define "excellent" visibility as 60 feet!

Our daily routine was to stay out on the boats for two morning dives and an afternoon dive. Lunch was sodas and sandwiches, although the boat crew would usually freedive to obtain two or three of the abundant local conchs, which they promptly made into fresh ceviche for us with their ever-present supply of tomatoes, onions, lime juice, and cilantro. On several days, we went ashore for lunch at a lovely stretch of pristine sand called San Francisco Beach. The islanders had erected two open-sided thatched-roof palapas for shade. With its broad expanse of sandy beach accented by palms, mangroves, hibiscus and other exotic plants, this was truly a tropical paradise. Our only companions here were the native great-tailed grackles, the tiny flitting swallows for whom the island was named, and the occasional lizard or iguana.

Of course, even paradise has its flaws, and Cozumel in 1974 was no exception. Out on the dive boats every day, when we finished our lunch and sodas, we carefully stashed our empty bottles and other trash in a corner where it wouldn't get blown or knocked overboard. And every day, the crew tidied up by taking said trash and throwing it overboard, straight into the waters of the reef! I shook my head and envisioned what the reefs would look like in 20 or 30 years, with hundreds of coral-encrusted soda bottles sprinkled about.

Over the intervening 39 years, our idyllic backwater paradise has burgeoned in population from 12,000 to over 100,000 people and has been transmogrified into a popular cruise ship destination with about one and a half million cruise ship visitors each year. We saw six full-sized cruise ships berthed along the waterfront, two per pier at each of the three major piers. Additionally, what used to be the town's one and only wharf has been greatly expanded to accommodate a fleet of large ferries that ply the waters between Cozumel and the mainland Yucatan 12 miles away several times daily.

Our charming Cabañas del Caribe (later renamed Sol Cabañas del Caribe) was completely destroyed by the category 5 Hurricane Wilma in 2005, and the coastline north of San Miguel is now lined with a dozen or more high-rise condos and vacation clubs. That miles-long stretch of pristine, uninhabited beach that ran half the length of the island south of town is now lined with mile after mile of timeshares, condos, and vacation clubs.

At San Francisco Beach, no vestige of the two palapas remain. The entire area is covered in bright-blue lounge chairs, a veritable forest of sun umbrellas sporting beer and other commercial logos and a large white tent where visitors can get their hair braided, skin tattooed with henna, or bodies massaged. In the beautiful aqua waters just off the beach, eight or ten large inflatable rafts and floating bounce houses in a variety of colors and shapes provide hours of entertainment for the mostly young visitors from the United States.

Even the windward side of the island, which had been completely uninhabited, is now dotted with at least eight restaurant/bar establishments, most of which play loud American rock music (I recognized SiriusXM's Classic Vinyl station at one place), serve gallons of beer to young American party crowds, and are surrounded by thickets of souvenir vendors' booths.

Much to our surprise and delight, given all these enormous changes, the reefs appeared practically unchanged from when we had first seen them, other than areas of coral rubble that evinced the double-whammy destructive power of Hurricanes Emily and Wilma in 2005. We found the reefs still covered in dozens of varieties of colorful sponges in all sorts of exotic shapes: vases, barrels, tubes, ropes, volcanoes, encrusting, and the ever-charming "lumpy" forms. We saw a wealth of corals, including gorgonians; sea fans; whips and rods; fingers; pillars; and mounds of brain, star, and maze corals. Algae, too, provided an abundance of their brown, green, and red accents to the reefs.

We had frequent encounters with the splashy queen angelfish and her more understated cousins, the French and gray angelfishes, butterflyfishes (always in pairs), parrotfish, trumpetfish, triggerfish, and the delightfully odd-shaped trunkfish. We even saw several good-sized groupers. As we cruised along a large open sandy area, we happened upon a southern stingray hanging out with a friendly jack. Occasionally, I would glance to the side to discover a large barracuda cruising along, eyeing me with suspicion. And much to my delight, we saw sea turtles on almost every dive: loggerheads, greens, and hawksbills.

My memories of soda bottles being flung into the ocean were still remarkably clear in my mind, and we had been witness over three decades to the degradation and depopulation of our own reefs and islands in California as the human population increased and diving, fishing, and pollution took their toll. We had seen what clear-cut logging and fertilizer-laden runoff had done to the previously clear waters off of Borneo. And we have read dozens of articles on the collapse of fish populations, coral reef die-offs, the Great Pacific Garbage Patch, and other environmental tragedies of recent decades.

But now in Cozumel, we didn't see any evidence of discarded soda bottles or other garbage! As it happens, in 1996, the entire reef system from Puerta Maya to Punta Chiqueros was designated as a national marine park, *Arrecifes de Cozumel National Park*.

Additionally, the museum in San Miguel includes exhibits that detail the formation and ecology of the reefs, the marine life inhabiting them, and the impact of human habitation and activities on the health and future of the reefs.

Cozumel is blessed with a very fortunate location in the Caribbean. The dominant ocean current is the Guiana Current, which flows clockwise up from South America. Because the Yucatan Channel is relatively narrow, the current flows faster as it passes the western coast of Cozumel, bringing in a constant supply of nourishment for the local corals and other sea life and washing away any sediments (and garbage) that might impede the sea life's growth and health. The island itself is porous, so rainwater seeps down into the large underground aquifer, rather than running off the island via rivers and streams. The local economy is largely tourist-based, so there is no large-scale farming, and most of the land is still covered in native vegetation. The *Cozumeleños* are very much aware of how exceptional their reefs are, from both an aesthetic and commercial (tourism) point of view, and are doing everything they can to preserve and protect them.

We celebrated our return to Cozumel with a gourmet dinner at La Cocay, which is ranked among the best restaurants on the island. (One of the silver linings that comes with the hordes of cruise ship tourists is a lively and healthy economy, including fine dining.)

In between courses, we chatted with our waiter, Esteban, who was probably in his mid-20s. Originally from Guadalajara, he came to

Cozumel with his then girlfriend. The two of them learned to dive, and although she did not like the island and ended up leaving, he has remained. There was a fire in his eyes and an intensity in his voice when he spoke about diving. He responded enthusiastically to our stories of the diving trips we have made over the years, and he fervently expressed his desire to have similar experiences. We met many other locals like him during our stay—young divers who love the ocean and care about its health and future.

The day before we left Cozumel, we visited Galeria Azul, a local art gallery just around the corner from La Cocay. The Galeria's owner is a local artist, Greg Dietrich, who specializes in incredibly beautiful blown and carved art glasswork and has recently started doing paintings on silk. Greg is an ex-pat from the United States who moved to Cozumel about 15 years ago when he fell in love with and married an equally talented local artist, Liliana Macotela.

As I browsed through the silk paintings, one in particular caught my eye. It was a fabulous lavender and yellow splendid toadfish on a red silk background.

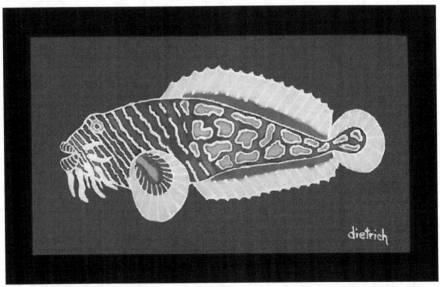

My Cherished Splendid Toadfish   Cozumel, Mexico
Painting by Greg Dietrich
Judith Hemenway Photo ©

That painting now hangs on our wall at home, where I can enjoy it every day. It serves as a constant reminder of the rare and beautiful treasures that are still being cherished and preserved on Cozumel today, in spite of all the growth and changes that have occurred over the past four decades.

I look at that vibrant painting every day, and I smile and say to myself, *Splendid. Simply Splendid.*

CHAPTER 27

THE CYCLE OF LIFE CONTINUES

Paul

Have you ever wondered why we are here, riding, in Jimmy Buffett's words, ". . . this big round ball"? What are we supposed to do during our time on Planet Ocean, which to an alien watching us from far out in the black void of space resembles a giant white and blue bubble circling a star?

A day at the beach helped me uncover one possible answer. In Chapter 5: Liquid Time Travel, I wrote:

> Since Carol and I were both beach lovers, we knew that we would instill an appreciation for ocean life in our children. Years later, watching our two little girls, Christine and Laura, walking ahead of us along the surf line, really opened my eyes to the almost supernatural hold the ocean has on children. They walked, skipped, and danced through the surf in a world of their own . . .

Fast forward to August 15, 2014.

We splash in the surf at Jones Beach, Long Island, with our grand-daughters Ava and Emma. I feel confident that I can say, "mission accomplished." The cycle of life will continue because both of our girls are passing their love of the ocean on to their children. Christine and Seth have introduced Max to the Atlantic Ocean at Point Lookout and Jones Beach, while Laura and Russ have dipped Emma's and Ava's toes into the Atlantic at Avalon, New Jersey.

Today, Carol, Laura, and I enjoy Ava and Emma at Jones Beach. I thrill standing next to Ava, just over two-and-a-half years old, as I watch her explore the wet sand for tiny treasures deposited by the incoming tide. Oyster, scallop, and muscle shells abound, some still intact, other shells crushed into tiny bits by the pounding ocean. I notice a few small pieces of sea glass glinting in the sun. A shiny, black "mermaid's purse" (a skate egg case) floats nearby. Tiny live mussels have attached themselves to its tendrils, gaining a free ocean ride. Seagulls buzz low overhead searching for an easy meal.

When Ava splashes into the surf, no sooner is she wading knee-deep than a crashing wave chases her back to shore in a cascade of white foam. As the spent wave retreats with the hiss of bursting bubbles and the soothing *clickity-clack* of tumbling sea shells, she scampers toward the water until another wave pushes her ashore again. Ava never tires or gets bored of this repeating cycle, as she runs, spins, and laughs, playing tag with Mother Ocean. But why should she? Every wave is different from the preceding one. One rises and curls, displaying an aqua-green hue just before it breaks, and then hurls the surf toward shore with exploding force. We feel more than hear a thumping *whump*. I stand close, ready in case Ava gets toppled, but she gamely holds her own. The next wave approaches and surges toward the beach, but this time the crest does not curl. It loses energy and then washes ashore, gently kissing Ava's toes. She giggles and points down as the receding water pulls the sand back, tickling her feet.

"Look, Paca." ("Grandpa" in Ava's unique language, which maturity will correct all too soon.) She squeals in delight.

Carol and Laura hold Emma's hands, letting her get a feel for the water. She smiles and laughs, all too eager to follow her big sister, but like her cousin Max, at one year old, she is not yet stable enough to challenge the ocean surf.

Their time will come soon enough, probably next summer. I can't wait! I look at our grandchildren, realizing they are the next generation, and I think about the world we will leave—our inheritance to them. I can only hope that these magical times we spend with them at the ocean will inspire a sense of wonder and awe and create a desire to explore and protect the sea and all its inhabitants. It looks like they are off to a good start.

CONCLUSION
Judy and Paul

Although we are both well into our 60s, neither one of us has any intention of giving up diving in the foreseeable future, so we're disinclined to think about conclusions. Continuations, yes. Conclusions, no.

It has been a privilege to explore beneath the waves, shiver over sharks, gaze into the eyes of whales, fly with eagle rays, listen to the sound of sand, come face-to-face with countless species of animals that we never dreamed existed, and explore history from a different perspective. We've traveled to the other side of the world, experienced different cultures, seen the Southern Cross, and appreciated the beauty of coral reefs.

The Profusion of Life on Amazing Rock
Judith Hemenway Photo ©

Solomon Islands

Not only that, but we've been lucky enough to enjoy these adventures in the company of our loved ones and friends.

There is still so much to see and explore and never enough time. Watching bubbles burble from a diver's regulator, shimmer and expand as they rise and end their short existence at the surface, reminds us that our lives are short.

So make the most of your time on our beautiful blue bubble, treat every day as a gift and take no day for granted. And always remember, *Bubbles Up!*

Turtle Bubble Bath on Cedral Wall   Cozumel, Mexico
Paul Mila Photo ©

ACKNOWLEDGMENTS

Judy

Almost all of the adventures I have described in these pages were shared with my husband Jon and were made possible by a remarkable fleet of dive boats with their skilled, dedicated, and companionable crews:

❖ In California, we have spent countless hours on the *Truth*, *Conception*, and *Vision*, all run by Truth Aquatics out of Santa Barbara, CA. (www.truthaquatics.com)

We have also enjoyed time on the *Peace* out of Ventura, CA (www.peaceboat.com), and we remember with great fondness the *Scuba Queen* (San Pedro, CA) and her skipper Pete Greenwood. Sadly, both the *Queen* and her skipper are no longer with us.

❖ In Papua New Guinea, the skipper and crew of the *Paradise Sport* introduced us to the marvels of muck diving. (Mike Ball Expeditions www.mikeball.com)

❖ In the Solomon Islands, the *Bilikiki* and her consistently amazing crew have twice provided us with outstanding diving adventures:

in 2004 with Divemasters Monty and Michelle and again in 2010 with Divemasters Sam and Kellie. (www.bilikiki.com)

❖ In the Dominican Republic on board the *Turks & Caicos Aggressor II* (aka the *TCA-II*), Skipper Piers van der Walt and Second Skipper Christopher Guglielmo and their crew provided our memorable first experiences with humpback whales. (www.aggressor.com/dominican.php)

❖ In Tonga, owner and skipper Rob Barrel of the *Naia* shared his wealth of knowledge of humpback whales with Jon, Paul, and I, and both Rob and his exceptional crew, along with trip coordinator Sonia Goggel, gave me compassion and support when I most needed it. (http://tinyurl.com/naia-whales)

In addition to these boats and their crews, there are other organizations and individuals who deserve special mention here:

❖ Over two decades ago, Divemaster Haris and the rest of the staff of the Borneo Divers resort introduced us to sea turtles and many other exceptional sea creatures on Sipadan Island. (www.sipadan.com/Borneo-Divers.php)

❖ In Cozumel, Paul's dive instructor Alison Dennis (www.scubawithalison.com) introduced me to the wonders of the splendid toadfish, and artist Greg Dietrich of Galleria Azul (www.cozumelglassart.com) captured that toadfish in color on silk for me to cherish.

And of course, beyond the adventures is the retelling of them in writing, which would not have happened without my coauthor, Paul, whose enthusiasm for diving and writing about diving provided the initial impetus (not to mention the title) for this book.

ACKNOWLEDGMENTS

Paul

An enthusiastic thank you to my friends and family who had a role in the creation of *Bubbles Up*, even though most of them never realized their contribution:

- ❖ Dive instructor Alison Dennis, owner/operator of *Scuba with Alison*, who introduced me to the amazing world under the sea.

- ❖ Coauthor Judy, who began this literary journey with me back in 2004 and along the way introduced me to the humpbacks in Tonga, South Pacific, and the gray whales in Baja California Sur.

- ❖ Tish Dace, for her encouragement and mentoring.

- ❖ Fulvio Cuccurullo, who arranged the Special Effects Dive and our meeting with the flying eagle rays of Cozumel.

- ❖ Martha Katz of Scuba Network of Long Island where I took my scuba training, who sold me on the idea that swimming with sharks was fun. (www.scubalongisland.com)

❖ Barbara Buchanan of Scuba Planners Dive Travel, for permission to use her quote.
(www.scubaplanners.com and www.fishtalesproductions.com)

❖ The many dive buddies and friends I have made during these years of diving, who shared many of these adventures with me, including Jamie and Jeff Margolies and their merry band of Diversified Divers, www.diversifieddivers.com, and Joe Troiano, who enjoys (or endures?) our annual Cozumel adventure.

❖ Miguel Núñez, for permission to use his photo of Nick Fittipaldi's 2000th dive. (www.cozumelimages.com)

❖ Dick Stuart, for permission to use his barracuda photo.

❖ Chuck Wade, for a great shark trip on the *Sea Turtle*.
(www.seaturtlecharters.com)

ACKNOWLEDGMENTS

Judy and Paul

❖ The adventures with the Atlantic humpback whales we have written about would not have been possible without the dedication and commitment of the government of the Dominican Republic, which established and maintains the Silver Bank Whale Sanctuary.

❖ Similarly, we are grateful to the Mexican government for maintaining protected breeding grounds in Baja California Sur for the Eastern Pacific gray whale population.

❖ And special thanks from us to Maria and Esther Mitrani of Andiamo Travel for their enthusiasm, knowledge, and love of the gray whales. Their ecotours to the lagoons play a significant role in educating the public on the current status of, and future hopes for, these extraordinary mammals. (www.andiamo-travel.com/?id=gray_whales)

❖ Both of us are particularly grateful to our editor Lorraine Fico-White of Magnifico Manuscripts. She constantly challenged us to rewrite our adventures and improve our storytelling. Her exceptional editing skills are matched by her patience and her vision of what our initial drafts could become. (www.magnificomanuscripts.com)

❖ Our thanks to Lorie DeWorken, who provided excellent interior layout and cover design services. Lorie was a pleasure to work with, and her creativity and enthusiasm helped make the project a success. (www.mindthemargins.com)

❖ Our appreciation also to our test readers, who patiently waded through the draft, and whose suggestions definitely improved the final product:

Bonnie Cardone, Fred Chiappetta, Sandi Constantino-Thompson, Tish Dace, Ben Davison, Jon Fellows, Wes Gavins, Robert Greco, Susan Harper, Melissa Holbert, Peter Katsumata, Karen Sunde, and Laura Wilkinson.

ABOUT JUDY HEMENWAY

Judy and Her Husband, Jon Fellows
Ready to Dive ©

Silver Bank Whale Sanctuary, Dominican Republic

As a young child, Judy was afraid of the water until the fateful day her father picked her up and threw her, water wings and all, into the deep end of the pool. She immediately realized she had found her true element and hasn't come out of the water since, except grudgingly to earn enough money to support her scuba diving habit.

She grew up in the farmlands of Pennsylvania with the inspiration of Hollywood classics such as *Flipper, Sea Hunt,* and *20,000 Leagues Under the Sea* and began diving in 1973, shortly after she moved to Southern California and met her soon-to-be husband. Since then, she has completed roughly 1,500 dives, ranging from her home waters in California to such exotic locations as: Cozumel and the Turks and Caicos Islands in the Caribbean; Mexico's Sea of Cortez and the Baja lagoons San Ignacio and Ojo de Liebre; the Melanesian island nations

Fiji, Papua New Guinea, and the Solomons; the Polynesian Kingdom of Tonga; Malaysian Borneo; and most recently, the Indonesian island Sulawesi.

Until her retirement a few years ago, Judy maintained a career as a network security engineer in Southern California. Judy and her husband currently reside on several acres among the native oaks and rolling vineyards of the Central Coast with their gopher-hunting cat Francisco, his deer-patrolling German shepherd sidekick Dexter, and two rescued desert tortoises, Trumble and Flatty.

When she is not diving or writing about diving, Judy goes wine tasting with family and friends, cultivates California native plants, and of course plots where she will travel next.

You can contact Judy via e-mail at judith@divingturtle.com and visit her website http://www.divingturtle.com and Facebook page https://www.facebook.com/JudithHemenwayAuthor.

ABOUT PAUL MILA

Paul Swimming with a Hawksbill Turtle
Photo Courtesy of Alison Dennis ©

Cozumel, Mexico

Paul Mila has expanded his horizons from Brooklyn to Baja and beyond. In 2002, he traded in his corporate suit for a wetsuit and now devotes his time to writing, scuba diving, underwater photography, and speaking to groups about ocean conservation.

He has enjoyed photographing and diving with Caribbean reef sharks in the Bahamas, humpback whales in the Dominican Republic and Tonga, and diverse sea life around the world, including his home waters of Long Island, New York.

Diving in the same waters as the characters in his books enables Paul to write exciting, realistic dive adventures and to accurately describe the beauty and wonder of our undersea world for non-diving readers.

Bubbles Up is his first dive into nonfiction writing.

Paul and his family reside in Carle Place, New York. When not diving, Paul writes thriller/adventure novels, works at a local dive shop, and coaches tennis. You can contact Paul via e-mail at paul@paulmila.com, visit his website at www.milabooks.com, and check out his newsletter, *The Sea-gram*, at www.sea-gram.com.